Curiosities Ser

D1622850

Missouri
CURIOSITIES

Quirky characters,
roadside oddities &
other offbeat stuff

Third Edition

Josh Young

Guilford, Connecticut

For my parents, who filled our home with laughter.

The prices, rates, and hours listed in this guidebook were confirmed at press time. We recommend, however, that you call establishments to obtain current information before traveling.

To buy books in quantity for corporate use
or incentives, call **(800) 962–0973**
or e-mail **premiums@GlobePequot.com.**

Copyright © 2010 by Morris Book Publishing, LLC

Photos by Josh Young unless otherwise noted.
Maps by Design Maps, Inc. copyright © Morris Book Publishing, LLC
Text design: Bret Kerr
Layout artist: Casey Shain
Project editor: John Burbidge

Library of Congress Cataloging-in-Publication data is available on file.

ISBN 978-0-7627-5864-7

Printed in the United States of America

contents

★ ★

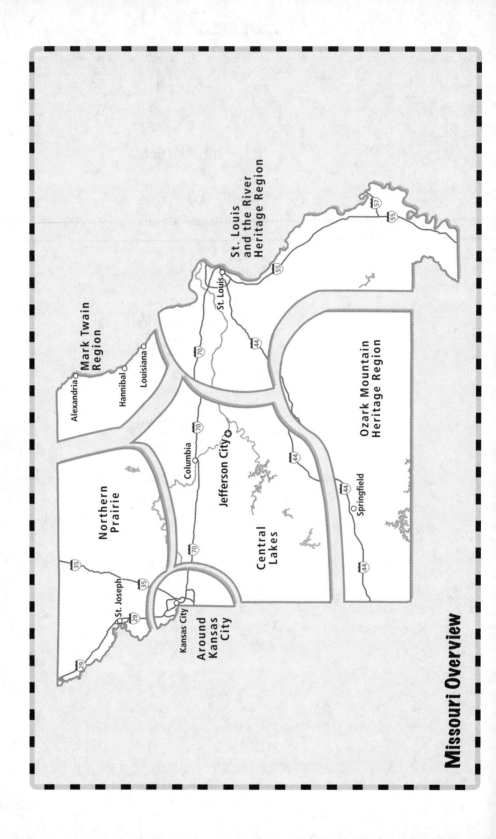

Missouri Overview

★ ★

Missouri is nicknamed the Show Me State (and if you read this book carefully, you'll find out why). But don't think for a minute that our nickname means that all you have to do is show up here and we will show you what Missouri is all about.

Sure there are some big attractions here that everybody visits or sees advertised. The Gateway Arch in St. Louis is probably the most famous man-made landmark in the Midwest. Branson has been called "the second most popular tourist destination in America" (after Disney World). We have hugely popular individual tourism sites, such as Bass Pro Shops Outdoor World, the Precious Moments attraction, and Meramec Caverns (made famous generations ago by barn signs and billboards along America's highways).

But the real Missouri is a little more hidden—beneath the notice of the casual traveler (and sometimes farther underground than Meramec Caverns). Learn the true meaning of "Show Me," and say it with conviction as you mosey around Missouri, and people here will reveal to you oddities and quirkiness you would not have expected in the "boring" middle Midwest.

Some of our secrets not even longtime Missouri residents know about. Like the 5- and 10-kilometer Groundhog Run, which takes place annually—entirely underground. (You are not likely to see that advertised anywhere because, although it is a hugely popular road race, the organizers get more than enough paid entrants signed up weeks in advance.)

Other Missouri curiosities are familiar to anyone who has lived here for a while, but they are not things that everybody talks about. Down around Joplin, almost everybody knows about the Spooklight. Most people have seen the eerie glowing balls more than once, but if you ask about it with the wrong attitude, you might suddenly feel as though you are in one of those episodes of *The Twilight Zone* where the whole town is in cahoots.

Signs that read SPOOKLIGHT ROAD were stolen so many times that they've been replaced with others that merely give county road designations. (In some cases the signs were simply not replaced at all.) But people thereabouts, like most other Missourians, are proud that they can claim one of the world's most studied—but still unexplained—phenomena. If you can muster a little Show Me pride, they may show you, too.

As I traveled the state researching this book, I met wonderful people who were eager to help. "Write about Miss Ella," they told me in northeast Missouri, where you might think there was nothing going on. "She was the tallest woman who ever lived, or something like that," was a common description, which inevitably ended by referring me to *Ripley's Believe It or Not!* for the essential details.

After all the waitresses and several patrons in a Bootheel cafe agreed, "You gotta meet Jake," an elderly woman scribbled a phone number down on her napkin and slipped it to me.

"And when you get over there by Columbia, give my brother a call," she said, clearly not wanting to be outdone. "You tell him Thelma told you to call and that he should tell you about that history for the book he has been writing. He knows so much about that area, you may never shut him up!"

A Show Me attitude got me into a tiny museum, only open part-time, where vast files of the uncataloged papers of famous American horticulturist Luther Burbank lie fallow. There is probably enough material there for two or three graduate students to earn their doctorates, but they will be wasting their time if they are searching for those documents in Burbank's native Massachusetts or in California, where the pioneer scientist did much of his research.

Artists are often great self-promoters, but Missouri sculptors Joey Los and Larry Vennard actually seemed surprised when I asked them to show me their creations. (The woman who told me about Larry's dinosaurs "just standing there, out on the farm," made them sound easier to find than they actually were, but I was glad I persisted until I found out where the heck his farm was.) Even the teenagers working at the fast-food joint a couple of miles away hadn't heard of Larry's dinosaurs, but I got the impression that when they got off work, they might just go by and check them out.

I got a lot of comments along the lines of, "No, I can't really think of anything odd or curious around here, except that our town square is supposed to be the second largest in this part of the state." Then, as I was walking out the door, they would say something like, "Of course there are the bed races we have every year; last year the county judge got caught cheating," or "I don't suppose your readers would be interested in the flying manure spreader?"

I hope you will use this book as a guide to get off the beaten track and away from the major tourist attractions to find some of Missouri's other wonders. Learn the concept of "Show Me," and find out what makes Missourians a little stubborn and so very different from the rest of the country. (We are the only state to have elected a dead governor to the U.S. Senate, remember.)

While you are out and about, see if you can learn the whereabouts of the grave for the dead circus elephant that was buried whole and memorialized by some small town in Missouri. I've heard it's out there somewhere—but I'm from Missouri.

You've got to show me.

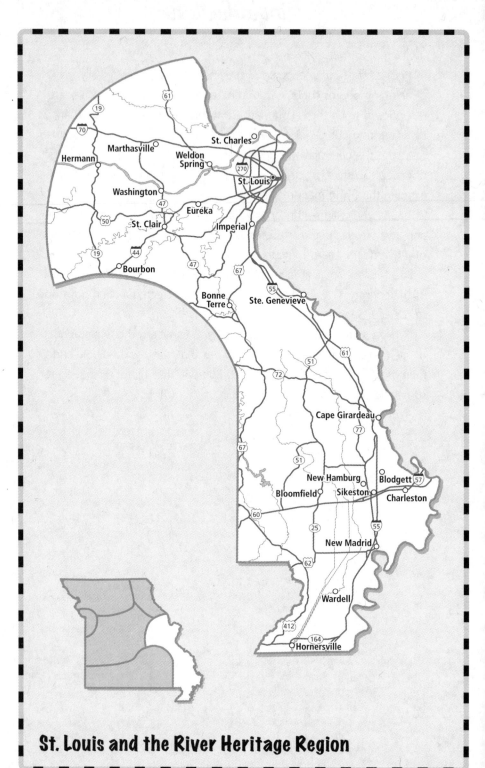

St. Louis and the River Heritage Region

1

St. Louis and the River Heritage Region

"First in shoes, first in booze, and last in the American League" was the flippant way people described St. Louis back when the St. Louis Browns were batting in the ballparks. In the years since, the shoe industry has taken a hike. But booze still rules, and the St. Louis Cardinals give the city a little more to cheer about.

That giant croquet wicket, the Gateway Arch, makes the St. Louis skyline instantly recognizable, and it's really pretty cool. If you want to test your courage, ride up inside the Arch some windy day to the observation room at the top, then lean with your belly flat on the outward sloping wall and peer down through one of the little windows. If the swaying motion doesn't make you queasy, faint—or a screaming maniac—you are probably Fear Factor material.

Never the seat of state government, St. Louis sometimes acts as if it were. Other communities in the state have to organize, cooperate, and lobby hard when they want to stop St. Louis from getting its own way at the expense of the rest of the state.

By comparison, this now-powerful metropolis was little more than a mudflat outpost when explorers Lewis and Clark camped and trained their men just across the river in Illinois during the winter of 1803. The famous pair launched their historic journey with a crossing at St. Louis in May 1804. A flood of settlers followed into the newly acquired Louisiana Purchase. Most pushed immediately westward, but tens of thousands stayed on in St. Louis to profit from the burgeoning river trade.

★ ★

Bridges were built to replace ferries as the common conveyance across the Mississippi, and the city's place in history was firmly set. State government moved from nearby St. Charles to Jefferson City, but St. Louis remained the tail that could wag the dog.

Today St. Louis and the surrounding communities are a rich mixture of cultures epitomizing the American melting pot. The city is world class and cosmopolitan yet midwestern and friendly, with small towns and farmland at its outer edges. Like any other thriving metropolis, St. Louis also boasts some pretty quirky stuff, both inside the city limits and downstream.

As you meander from St. Louis south, you will see that nowhere else in Missouri is the influence of early Spanish and French settlement as pronounced as along the Mississippi River in southeast Missouri. The architecture here is some of the most beautiful in the state and attests to a long history of prosperity and growth. Steamboat trade dominated many river towns, even after railroads reached them. In towns like Cape Girardeau, the history of river commerce is on proud display. A wave of German immigration followed, and today the social fabric of these communities is more German than either Spanish or French.

The town of New Madrid came early under American influence. Immediately following the Revolutionary War, Col. George Morgan received a grant of fifteen million acres of contested Spanish land, creating a buffer of sorts between Spanish territory and the newly established United States. Morgan persuaded many settlers to move to the New Madrid area, where many were dubiously "privileged" in 1811 to experience what was perhaps the most violent earthquake ever recorded in North America.

Missouri's "bootheel" came about more quietly in 1821, at the time of the Missouri Compromise. Area residents were unwilling to wait for statehood to reach Arkansas and benefit them, so the border was finagled south. The jog took a chunk out of the future state of Arkansas—and gained statehood status for the Bootheel area fifteen years earlier than it would have otherwise.

Over the River and Through the Woods

Blodgett

Once upon a time, in fact well into the twentieth century, the United States had a predominantly agricultural economy. So those people who didn't live on farms probably had a relative who did. Children could visit and gather the eggs. Nowadays a disturbing number of kids can't tell you where milk comes from, other than out of the dairy case at the supermarket.

Even Lewis and Clark could get lost here.
MISSOURI DIVISION OF TOURISM

Beggs Family Farm is like going to Grandpa and Grandma's farm—if they owned the biggest operation in twelve counties and let you play on almost everything.

Established in 1895, and kept in the same family ever since, Beggs Farm began as a watermelon farm, and for several years the family could boast of being the biggest melon grower in the state of Missouri. That was quite an accomplishment in Blodgett, which officials at the 1904 World's Fair declared "the Watermelon Capital of the World."

In melon season, freight trains transporting the fruit from Blodgett used to stretch for more than a mile. With wide fluctuations in market prices, however, back then an entire year's crop might go unsold and instead be fed to the hogs.

Today the lines stretching into Beggs Farm bring eager families by the carload to experience U-pick strawberries, Easter egg hunts, hayrides, farm animal displays, and an annual twelve-acre corn maze. (To celebrate the 200th anniversary of the Lewis and Clark Expedition, the Beggs Family Farm let visitors get lost in a maze representing the Journey of Discovery.)

Clever rides and playground equipment represent all aspects of farming, so everyone can share in a fun farm experience like Grandma and Grandpa used to give.

The still-working farm is open to the general public seasonally; fees vary. Throughout the year the farm is open to school groups and others on field trips, with advance reservations.

The Beggs Family Farm is 6 miles north of Sikeston, at exit 69 off I-55. Call (573) 471-3879 or visit www.beggsfamilyfarm.com for information.

Really Fast Food
Bloomfield

Bloomfield was once little more than a way station through the heavy forests and swamps of southeast Missouri. What little transport there was through the region was done on flatboats, where possible, or along rough roads that had been Indian trails not long before.

The forests have been cleared and most of the swamps drained, but this is still horse and cattle country. Every year on Memorial Day weekend, folks gather to celebrate their heritage (or to get a clue of what kind of wild pioneers made the land livable for modern-day transplants). The event is the annual Rodeo & Chuckwagon Races, held at the Holly Ridge Ranch just outside town.

Sixty-five teams of horses and mules, often with a driver still clinging to the reins, compete at breakneck speed in such categories as "buckboard" and "classic wagon." Although even the rigs that finish

Food just can't get to you any faster than by chuck wagon.
MISSOURI DIVISION OF TOURISM

★ ★

Trivia

While in Bloomfield, stop by the Stars and Stripes Museum and Library. The famous military newspaper was founded and originally published here.

flat last probably maintain speeds faster than the driver of your last home pizza delivery, the notion that chuck wagons raced to their destinations is no doubt a false one. For the most part those early teamsters were transporting cargo, slowly and carefully, to avoid broken axles and wheels hub deep in mud.

Still it's fun to see what speed and agility modern wagoners can coax from their spirited animals. Other events round out the weekend into a very enjoyable rodeo, but the chuck wagon races are what everybody comes to see and goes away talking about.

If you get a hankering for some good food but can't find anybody serving out of the back of his Conestoga, the Cowtown Cafe, at the Holly Ridge Ranch, is a fine place to eat. They serve meals on weekends year-round, specializing in catfish and steaks. Their hush puppies are shut-your-mouth good.

Bloomfield is north of US 60 on MO 25, between Poplar Bluff and Sikeston. Take State Route E east out of Bloomfield for about a mile to get to the Holly Hill Ranch. For information on the Rodeo & Chuckwagon Races, call (573) 568-3157 (weekends only).

A Lake Like No Other

Bonne Terre

So you say you would like to go to the lake—maybe swim, go boating, or just walk along the shore. But you hate putting on all that sunscreen, the lake is always crowded, and what if a storm comes up and spoils your plans?

The place for you is Bonne Terre Mine, a remarkably little-known National Historic Site and home of what has been called the largest underground lake in the world.

Winter or summer, stormy or bright, the water in Bonne Terre Mine is always 58 degrees, and the temperature of the surrounding air doesn't vary from 62 degrees. All this is possible because

Still waters really do run deep at Bonne Terre.
MISSOURI DIVISION OF TOURISM

you are in an abandoned lead mine that covers 80 square miles in five levels. Operated for nearly one hundred years, until the 1960s, by the St. Joe Lead Company, the mine had been a much smaller surface lead mine for decades prior to that. After Bonne Terre Mine was abandoned, with much of the old equipment still inside, water slowly seeped in, creating the huge body of still waters that run so deep today. In 1981 Doug and Cathy Goergens acquired commercial rights to operate dives and underground tours, and thus was born what *National Geographic* has listed as one of America's top-ten adventures.

Divers love the experience because of the 100-foot visibility, the unique setting, and more than half a million watts of lights that subtly illuminate the twenty-four dive trails. Average dive depths range from 40 to 60 feet, passing through massive chambers, past calcium falls, and down old elevator shafts. Safety is enhanced by the ratio of two guides per ten divers and the lack of unpredictable currents sometimes encountered by divers in open water. (Dive lessons can be arranged too.)

Less-hardy souls will still feel adventurous taking the hour-long guided walking tour along the old mule trail at the water's edge. Today the mine entrance is through the same small building that mules once were led through on a one-way trip to work the rest of their lives down below—you'll get to go home.

A fun way to see the underground lake without going underwater is by taking a boat tour, which also includes a walking tour. The extraordinary visibility allows boat passengers to view many of the same features and artifacts that divers see.

Whether you go into the water or stay above it, back on the surface you can make arrangements to stay a little longer, either in the luxurious rooms and train car accommodations of the 1909 Depot or at the less fancy Diver's Lodge at the Mine. (Reservations are recommended.) For more information call (888) 843-3483 or visit www.2dive.com.

Shining Shoes above the Bootheel

Cape Girardeau

Long before he was polishing his acerbic radio wit against liberals and their causes, conservative talk show host Rush Limbaugh was shining shoes in the College Barber Shop in Cape Girardeau. Although he was only thirteen at the time, Rush doubtless enjoyed the extra spending money. This was not a poor boy's job of necessity; the Limbaugh name is synonymous with lawyers, wealth, and conservative politics in southeast Missouri.

Grampa Rush H. Limbaugh Sr. was ambassador to India during the Eisenhower administration. The radio Rush most people know is Rush H. Limbaugh III; his brother, David, who does his legal work, is with the firm founded by their grandfather. Uncle Stephen Limbaugh was appointed to the federal bench by Ronald Reagan, and cousin Stephen Jr. accepted a seat on the Missouri Supreme Court.

Rush's dad was reportedly not happy when his son chose a radio career instead of law or some other profession, but the controversial radio star has proven that talk show hosts can generate the same amount of love and money as lawyers.

While doing his shoeshine stint in the early 1960s, the littlest Rush got a reputation for imitating voices and telling stories. Those performances gave way to Rush's first gig as a teenage DJ. At local KGMO radio Rush got his start using the on-air name of Rusty Sharpe. A series of jobs with other radio stations around the country followed in a career even some of Limbaugh's admirers have called "checkered." Eventually the Duke of Dittoheads became nationally syndicated and world famous. But however big he gets, for a long time yet you will be able to find people around Cape Girardeau who can honestly say, "Rush Limbaugh used to shine my shoes."

★ ★

One Barber, Worth the Big Weight

Charleston

When a fella wants a good coiffure in southeast Missouri, he could do worse than wait for Henry Coffer. Proof of the number of men and boys who have been willing to do so was verified on December 8, 2008, when the *Guinness World Records* people confirmed that the barber's accumulated 167-pound ball of hair was the biggest they had ever recorded. (Clearly those Guinness folks never babysat my cat.)

When *Ripley's Believe It or Not!* sniffed out the story, they bought the ball for an undisclosed amount plus a lifetime pass for Henry to any of the Ripley's museums, worldwide.

Six months had transpired between the time Henry submitted his entry to Guinness and the day Ripley's took the thing off his hands, so by then Ripley's said the hairball weighed in at slightly over 170 pounds. It is hard to say where you have to go to see Henry's hairball—reportedly it will become one of Ripley's traveling exhibits. That's okay; I believe I'll pass.

The project got started years ago when one of Coffer's customers asked for a few hair clippings to spread around in his melon patch in hopes of deterring wild critters. When the gardener no longer needed any more hair, Henry just kept on collecting. I am not sure if a little hair sprinkled around in my garden would scare off rabbits, but just the sound of a giant hairball gives me the willies.

Hair or no hair, none of Coffer's many customers seem in the least put off by Henry, or his giant hairball. The first time I tried to talk to him, he had one customer in his chair and two waiting, and he said "after work" he was going over to a nursing home, where he was giving some haircuts for free. (Shhhhh . . .)

Coffer is the only barber serving several communities for miles around, so as he approaches his eightieth birthday, he remains in high demand. And he shows no signs of slowing down. Born in 1931, Henry went to barber college when flattops ruled. In the years since, he has seen plenty of hairstyles come and, ergo, hair go.

"That flattop was the toughest haircut to get right," he told me in a rare serious moment, "so I practiced that one until I got very good at it. I can do all the others," he said, not boasting.

When asked which haircut he likes to do least, he hemmed a bit before saying, "I never cared much for the way those DA's looked, but I can cut 'em. You know, those ones where, in the back, it looks like a duck waddling away from you?" (Children, can you say, "ducktail"?)

There's no disappointment in visiting Henry Coffer's Barber Shop. He's got the biggest barber pole ever sold as standard equipment. (Henry's is the classic red and white, from back before they started sticking blue on them.)

He's definitely not the kind of barber who will always have the same spiel when you sit down. You won't get, "Some weather we've been having, ain't it?" or "Been catching any fish lately?" from Henry.

"You may not always like the haircut I give you," he told me, unconvincingly, "but if I don't send you away laughing, I haven't done my job."

Henry, you're a pro.

Henry Coffer's Barber Shop is at 1115 South Main Street, open Monday through Friday 8:00 a.m. to 4:00 p.m. Follow the sound of laughter.

Trivia

The dogwood on Henry Coffer's place shares the state record for the biggest dogwood tree in Missouri. (I checked. The other one is a little fatter; Henry's is taller and almost as big around.)

All the Better to Protect You With

Eureka

Not all the important work done to save wolves happens out West and up North. For more than thirty years, since being founded by *Wild Kingdom*'s Marlin Perkins and his wife, the Wild Canid Survival and Research Center has bred, studied, and released endangered species of wolves back into the wild. Additionally, the WCSRC Wolf Sanctuary serves an important function by educating the public and dispelling myths that threaten wolf survival. And you get to howl.

Little Red Riding Hood, for example, was probably less in peril in the storybooks than the red wolf has been in America. The Wolf Sanctuary long led the successful effort to increase the population of the red wolf in this country. Now they've shifted their focus to accomplishing the same goal with the Mexican gray wolf. The Wolf Sanctuary is also one of the few places in the world to house maned wolves from South America.

The Wolf Programs take place at night. First you see a slide-and-film presentation about wolves, and you can ask a lot of questions. Next you walk (a half-mile round-trip) to an area near the wolf enclosures, where you'll be encouraged to howl at the top of your lungs. Usually that sets off a chorus from the real wolves that's guaranteed to raise the hair on the back of your neck. When the singing is over, the humans return to the center for refreshments and the opportunity to discuss what they have seen and heard.

This is a rare opportunity to get close to breeding populations of large carnivores, many of which are destined to be set free. The center annually hosts approximately 40,000 visitors ranging from schoolchildren to internationally renowned scientists, but interaction with humans is minimized to increase the wolves' chances of survival in the wild someday.

Not surprisingly, the center's most popular night is Halloween, so make your reservations early. Inappropriate costumes would include Little Red Riding Hood, Playboy Bunnies, or any of the Three Little Pigs.

Howl along with the wolves.
RUSSEL LAMPERTZ

Once you have your reservations, take exit 269 off I-44 west of St. Louis. For information, fees, and schedules, call the Wild Canid Center at (636) 938–5900 or visit www.wildcanidcenter.org. Reservations are required at least two weeks in advance, except for the annual open house, held a single Sunday in October.

The Best of the Wurst

Hermann

Where can you go where the wurst is the best, tying a brat has nothing to do with restraining unruly children, and nobody eats their favorite wiener dogs? Hermann, the "Sausage Capital of Missouri," offers all this and more every March.

You could do worse than swinging sausages with the Wurstjaeger Dancers.
STONE HILL WINERY

You'll find bratwurst, leberwurst, schwartenmagen, and sommer sausage to sample and buy. Then listen to traditional German music and watch the Wurstjaegers (German folk dancers) trip the light fantastic while swinging sticks laden with sumptuous sausages. Or enjoy a Sunday "whole hog sausage breakfast" and watch or compete in the sausage stuffing and tying competition.

Another favorite part of the Hermann Wurstfest is the annual "Wiener Dog Derby," where dachshund owners can race their doggies in the "Derby Dash," flaunt their fidos in the fashion show, and parade their puppies in the "Longest Wiener Dog Contest."

To reach Hermann take I-70 west of St. Louis to Danville, then go south on MO 19, past Big Spring. The festival is generally held the fourth weekend in March. For contest and lodging information, visit www.visithermann.com or call (800) 932-8687.

Lucy Ricardo Made It Look So Easy

Hermann

Instead of just lying around complaining about the heat in August, why not run on over to Hermann to participate in the annual Great Stone Hill Grape Stomp? Guides will be giving half-hour tours of the 1847 winery and its cool underground cellars, which took twenty-two years to construct. An American architectural wonder that's on the National Register of Historic Places, the cellars at Stone Hill are fascinating to tour any time of the year. They just feel better on a hot day in August.

Stone Hill is Missouri's most awarded winery. Before Prohibition ended its first great run, it was actually the third largest winery in the world.

If the winery tour doesn't do it, the Grape Stomp will definitely cool your heels. For a few dollars you can kick off your shoes and compete in the "Grand Stomp-Off" and the "Grand Style Stomp-Off." (In one you get judged on the amount of juice you generate; in the other you get judged on your costume and technique.) Less-ambitious visitors (or would-be contestants who don't arrive early enough) can pay a smaller fee to leave their shoes on, sit back, relax, and watch the fun as the fruit flies.

The event is held the second Saturday in August, and all proceeds

Delightfully Dancing at the Oddball

Joey Los isn't your average midwestern gal. The artist's hand-lettered and illustrated business card proudly proclaims, "No Job Too Odd!" In promoting her eclectic, earth-friendly metal sculptures, murals, portraits, and crazy creations she simply calls "objects," Joey consistently lives up to her promise to create "treasures from trash."

The daughter of a truck-driving auctioneer in a little town just outside St. Louis, Joey was raised a Buddhist, and the family's home was visited by a never-ending stream of interesting people from all over the world.

While still playing amid the normal truck and plunder found lying around a farm town auction barn, Joey remembers assembling mobiles from auction leftovers. In school she excelled in art.

Life took Joey on a little detour when she lived for several years in the Netherlands and returned to farm in Missouri with her husband and young son. On the farm it made perfect sense for Joey to take up the practical skill of welding. Her enjoyment of farm welding helped nudge her back to school to pursue art full-time.

from the Grape Stomp go to charity. In Hermann take Fifth Street to the top of the hill. You can't miss the winery. For more information visit www.stonehillwinery.com or call (573) 486-2221 or (800) 909-9463.

But at heart Joey was still the little girl who loved to pull stuff out of junk piles. At the University of Missouri in Columbia, she wove a huge—and hugely popular—interactive rubber tunnel sculpture from truck tires. Becoming, in her own words, "the trash queen," Joey eventually moved to Hermann, where she lives in an old house that was once a blacksmith's home.

From her small studio Joey cranks out a parade of figures, existing in her mind and manifested in steel. "Each piece is a celebration of life overlapping," she says, "unrelated items welded together into a harmonious whole like life itself." Odd birds, crooning frogs, ancient saguaro cacti, whimsical crawdads, wacky fish, and amazing acrobats spill out of Joey's mind and studio, delighting people and gracing their surroundings. A work of compass plants is installed in the Whitney Wildflower Garden.

Joey likes to quote sculptor Alexander Calder, who said, "My work is also my play." Those seem to be words Joey lives by. Now what is so odd about that?

Current works by Joey Los can always be seen at the Kunstlerhaus Gallery and Pottery Shop, 207 East First Street in Hermann. Or visit www.joeylos.com.

★ ★

Who's That Little Kid Smoking a Cigar?
Hornersville

That was no little kid. Back in the late 1800s, W. H. "Major" Ray was a midget who worked for the Sells Brothers Circus. For a time the 3-foot-6-inch Major Ray and his 37-inch-tall wife, Jennie, were billed as "the World's Smallest Couple." Around the turn of the twentieth century, they left the circus and bought a general store in Hornersville. Like virtually all other general stores at that time, the Rays' store inventory included Buster Brown Shoes.

Major Ray was picked to personify the little boy comic-strip character Buster Brown for the Brown Shoe Company at the 1904 St. Louis World's Fair, becoming the first of literally hundreds of children and "little people" to play the part of Buster Brown over the next several decades. Comic-strip pioneer R. F. Outcault sold the rights to use the Buster Brown image to about 200 companies at the World's Fair, but the Buster Brown Shoe Company is the most successful of those marketing matchups—and the one people most remember. Buster Brown Shoes are still sold today.

As for Major Ray, he had to dress in a waistcoat with short pants, a shirt with a big round collar, a large bow tie, and a wide-brimmed hat. This style was credited with getting little boys out of the dresses and smocks that infants and young children had traditionally been clothed in. The popularity of the Buster Brown "look" continued for decades, as you will notice the next time you watch a Little Rascals movie.

Major Ray retired from the Buster Brown biz not too long after the World's Fair and stayed in Hornersville for the rest of his life. He died in 1936 at the relatively advanced age of seventy-six. A monument was erected over his grave, showing Ray in Buster Brown clothing with his dog, "Tige," at his side.

Take It, Sheryl!

After winning her first seven Grammy awards, Kennett native Sheryl Crow was given an honorary doctorate from Southeast Missouri State University in recognition of her lifetime achievements, which include teaching music to autistic children in St. Louis before she left in 1986 to pursue her singing career.

In her inspirational speech to the 513 graduates assembled, Dr. Crow, music woman, is quoted as having said, "I know your sacrifices, and I have no words of wisdom, but I'm reminded of what Yogi Berra used to say when he found a fork in the road. 'Take it!'"

If You Kill It, You've Got to Clean It

Imperial

If it had been left up to me, we would still have mastodons lumbering around like they did just over 10,000 years ago. But then again, I get tired of turkey after the third day; I can't imagine how difficult it would be to come up with fresh new ways to cook the rump roast of a big, hairy elephant after a month without refrigeration. The ancient Native Americans must have been regular Martha Stewarts with the fire pit and spit when it came to mastodons, because they seem to have eaten every last one—that is, every one that didn't blunder into the Kimmswick mineral springs swamp and get turned to stone for our modern-day viewing pleasure.

If you are into this (and what nine-year-old isn't?), visit Mastodon State Historic Site and see all the displays of specimens and ancient artifacts, which remind us that the St. Louis area wasn't always shopping malls and expressways. They've got life-size dioramas, reconstructed mastodon skeletons, fossils, and artifacts from when early Americans hunted mastodons with stone-tipped spears. The Kimmswick Bone Bed is one of the biggest Pleistocene fossil deposits in North America, and scientists from all over the world come here to study the remnants of creatures that became trapped in the mineral-rich mud, which preserved them extremely well as they slowly petrified.

To go on your very own mastodon hunt, drive twenty minutes south of St. Louis on either I-55 or US 61 to Imperial. Mastodon State Historic Site is well marked at 1050 Charles J. Becker Drive. Call (636) 464-2976.

Getting Down and Dirty along the Big Muddy
Marthasville

There's a slew of slop and sludge slung in the slough every June when the Mid-Missouri Off-Roaders organize the annual Marthasville Spring Mud Bog.

How can you not have fun when you combine big boys (and girls), their tricked out 4-by-4s, and mud up to your rearview mirrors? Flood a huge trench, churn it up a little, and you've got a regulation bog track and a ticket to gloppy good times.

Driving rigs with names such as "Mud, Sweat, and Gears," "Fool Injected," "Gone Postal," and the nowadays obligatory "Git-R-Done," these Dukes of Dirt compete in events like "deep bog," "shallow drag," and side-by-side racing (in more mud of course).

Think you can't compete? With seven classes ranging from "everyday street vehicles" to "highly modified mud machines," almost anything you drive can carry you to muddy immortality or sink your cylinders in primordial ooze.

If you are too persnickety to get grit in the gearbox of your Navigator by competing, you can take in the Mud Bog as a spectator sport. I'd advise against wearing your Sunday best, however, as even casual observers are likely to get splattered as the little monsters maneuver through the mud with their big tires and souped-up engines.

Oh, and don't be put off by the gnarly looks of some of the club members and their rigs. Like most big, tough guys, these fellas are all soft and sweet inside. They use proceeds from their various events throughout the year to award an annual college scholarship, adopt families for Thanksgiving and Christmas, and sponsor a Little League team. They'll even put on a charity event for your organization (as long as you don't expect them to replace your lawn).

The Marthasville Spring Mud Bog is held the second Saturday in June each year. From exit 193 off I-70 west of St. Louis, take MO 47 south to Marthasville. Attendance and entrance fees are charged. For more information visit www.mmor.com.

Get down and dirty.
JIM OTT, MID-MISSOURI OFF-ROADERS

★ ★

The Rest of This Big One Got Away

Rick Crane was hoping for a big one when he went fishing over to Caruthersville awhile back. The Kennett resident noticed what he thought was an unusual-looking rock on the bank of the Mississippi. Being from a place where rocks are something of a novelty, Crane took the thing home and cleaned the mud off it. The more he studied it, the more the object fascinated him, so Rick took his find to the Pink Palace Museum in Memphis, where experts told him it was a tooth from a mastodon that probably lived some 20,000 years ago. A Southeast Missouri State University professor confirmed that opinion.

Allowing for inflation, how much do you suppose the Tooth Fairy would leave you if you put a mastodon tooth under your pillow?

A Load of Baloney
New Hamburg

Schindler's Tavern has atmosphere. You can't help having atmosphere in a building that dates back to at least 1848. The tavern itself was in the Schindler family for 131 years, and the owners since have done their utmost to preserve the spirit of the place. In a recent remodeling job, the old grill where the baloney burgers are cooked was retained to preserve the atmosphere and aromas. Still hanging around on one wall is the 6-foot-10-inch stuffed gar caught in 1912—its longevity no doubt enhanced by the eau d'baloney in the air.

People come from all across America to bite into a baloney burger, once they've heard there is such a thing. New owners Rick and

Heather Lawson say some people order a "double," but "that's more than most people can handle." The flavors and the fun crowd keep people coming back for more.

To seek out Schindler's, take I-55 south from Cape Girardeau to the Scott City exit. Then follow US 61 south approximately 7 miles through Kelso to State Route A. Turn right and go exactly 2 miles. Bring your appetite and a thirst. Call (573) 545-3709.

Playing Them as They Lie
New Hamburg

Almost anything is legal in the Kowpasture Klassic, a goofy annual 9-hole golf tournament held every year for charity in this town famous for baloney burgers. If the judges decide against you the first time you ask for a ruling, wait until the Beer Buggy makes another pass, and then ask them again. They may be in a more receptive mood.

The official balls of the K. P. Klassic are of the tennis type, and sanctioned clubs have included golf clubs, baseball bats, and wooden legs. The course is laid out on twenty-five acres of ruminant-roamed land behind Schindler's Tavern belonging to St. Lawrence Parish. Four-person teams pay $100 each to compete for the coveted satin victory jackets. Almost as coveted are the postgame sanctions for cheating, which seems to be encouraged by the judges, players, and rowdy bystanders.

Back in the mid-1980s, the first such fun fund-raiser was held to help send two local boys to the Kenny Rogers Cerebral Palsy Center in Sikeston. Other recipients since those two first honorees graduated from high school include the Missouri Veterans Home, the National World War II Memorial, and the Make-A-Wish Foundation.

The Kowpasture Klassic takes place each year on a weekend soon after Easter. Call Schindler's Tavern at (573) 545-3709 for details.

Like a Rock

Eventually the mighty Mississippi will claim everything in its path, but one thing that is taking a little longer to succumb than one might expect is Tower Rock. First recorded by French explorer Father Jacques Marquette in 1673, Tower Rock was dedicated to God in 1698, when three missionaries made their way to it, climbed to the top, and planted a cross. (This feat, presumably done in long woolen robes, also marks one of the earliest examples of Extreme Evangelical Sports.)

Lewis and Clark were impressed that the one-acre chunk of limestone was so stubbornly resisting the Mississippi's eroding waters; they surveyed the rock in 1803 and recorded its height as 92 feet. The explorers also noted that just navigating around the huge rock was a difficult obstacle to their journey because the sheer volume of it created an immense eddy in the river.

In 1839 more than 700 freedom-seeking German Lutherans passed by Tower Rock and made contact on their way to found the Lutheran Church Missouri Synod. This has caused Tower Rock to be informally known to some as "the Plymouth Rock of the Missouri Synod," a denomination with millions of members in North America.

Gen. Ulysses S. Grant seems to have developed some nostalgic fondness for Tower Rock's resistance in the face of its relentless enemy, the river. As a general, Grant several times guided his troops past Tower Rock, so he knew exactly what he was preserving when, as president, he refused to allow the Army Corps of Engineers to carry out a plan to blow the bluff to smithereens. Now Tower Rock is preserved as a National Landmark.

To see it yourself, go east on State Route A from Uniontown, through Frohna and Altenburg. Five miles past Altenburg and a half mile before the river, a small sign on the right points to Tower Rock. (If you begin to doubt the way, 2 miles out of Altenburg you will see Tower Rock Winery; you can stop there for additional inducements to go on.) A thirty-two-acre forest, including a 10-mile hiking trail, is associated with the lasting limestone landmark.

For more information call the Missouri district forest office at Cape Girardeau (573-290-5730).

Whole Lotta Shakin', Whole Lotta Holes

New Madrid

Forget California. Alaska has barely moved. The worst recorded earthquake in North American history took place in New Madrid—or at least where New Madrid used to be—just over a decade into the nineteenth century. Whereas the San Francisco earthquake of 1906 affected 60,000 square miles, the New Madrid jolts affected 1 million square miles—an area sixteen times greater.

"The Big One" was actually a series of earthquakes, mainly occurring from December 16, 1811, through February 7, 1812. The largest of these, an estimated 8.5 on the Richter scale, was violent enough to ring church bells in Boston and elsewhere on the East Coast. The tremors were felt all the way to the Rocky Mountains, Canada, and Mexico. Part of what was then Missouri broke away and moved to Kentucky. Five towns (in three states) were swallowed up. Buildings in St. Louis sustained structural damage. Islands in the Mississippi disappeared, and new lakes were formed on what had been solid ground. For a short time, the Mississippi River flowed backward.

The damage and loss of life would have been much worse if the region had not been so sparsely populated. Reports described horrible smells and dark vapors filling the air. There was a constant roar as the river claimed collapsing banks. Over that noise could be heard the bawling of animals and incessant human screams.

The very name of Pemiscot County, south of New Madrid in extreme southeastern Missouri, comes from the Indian word meaning "liquid mud." This is supposedly because the New Madrid earthquakes turned solid ground into a swampy morass overnight. Sand boils—geysers of sand and water from deep in the earth—shot up more than 100 feet in the air. (Areas where sand boils occurred almost 200 years ago still lie, infertile, in farmers' fields. One particularly active scene of sand boil activity is now a 139-square-mile region near the town of Deering, enthusiastically known to midwestern geology students longing for spring break as "the Beach.")

Experts differ as to the size and likelihood of future catastrophes, but everyone agrees that when the earth keeps moving as it does here, something's got to give. State and federal governments have disaster plans focusing on such an event, and road and building codes are continually reviewed and debated.

Back in 1990, late climatologist Iben Browning predicted a 50/50 chance of a major earthquake near New Madrid between December 1 and 5. He based his prediction on a series of factors, including the gravitational pull of the moon. Although experts dismissed Browning's predictions, major media attention caused a big brouhaha, ranging from serious preparedness drills to macabre earthquake-watch parties. The designated days came and went, leaving some people relieved, others feeling better prepared, and many just hung over. Thrift shops in the Bootheel area are good places to hunt for souvenirs proclaiming that you survived the 1990 earthquake.

The best place to investigate the scientific and historic sides of the New Madrid earthquake is at the New Madrid Historical Museum, 1 Main Street. Call (573) 748-5944 or visit www.newmadridmuseum.com for details.

Crank It Up
St. Louis

As a little boy crowding around his family's 1938 Philco radio with his four siblings, Jasper Giardina had a dream. "One of these days, we'll have a radio in every room!" he promised them, with confidence that must have sounded crazy at the time.

Jasper not only made that crazy dream come true, but he also didn't stop there. Now more than seventy years old, Jasper has amassed a collection of more than 10,000 radios. Jasper's Antique Radio Museum is a walk through the entire history of radio communications, representing radios from the late 1800s to the present. Homemade crystal sets take their place alongside valuable wireless

A Tower by Any Other Name

It certainly looks as if many Missourians don't want to get just plain water out of their taps. Evidence the old Bourbon tower in (where else?) Bourbon, Missouri, which has had travelers stopping with their cameras (and glasses) for years. Not to be outdone, St. Clair, farther up I-44 toward St. Louis, labeled their two prominent water towers "Hot" and "Cold." Then there is Tipton, over toward Sedalia on US 50, which has a big eight ball for a water tower (Fischer pool tables used to be manufactured there.) The town of Licking used to have a baseball water tower in honor of a local citizen who invented a machine that stitches baseballs, but when the Rawlings company left town, the tower reverted to just storing generic H_2O.

Despite appearances, you'll get just plain water from the Bourbon water tower.

radios from the 1920s. Jasper's favorite, a 1928 Atwater Kent bread-board radio, is so named because the parts are simply attached to a flat board, with no decorative cabinet.

Visitors to the museum get a kick out of the coin-operated radios, which play five or ten minutes for a nickel, like a jukebox. An even stranger radio, built by Westinghouse, was designed in a round cabinet to sit atop the rounded frame of a Westinghouse refrigerator. Jasper says he never throws a radio away because "there's no such thing as a bad radio." Only bad programming, I guess.

Jasper's Antique Radio Museum and Tropical Fruit Baskets is located at 2022 Cherokee Street. Admission is charged. For more information call (314) 421-8313.

Feel Like a Kid Again
St. Louis

The director of the Smithsonian Institution said, "Wow . . . we are speechless." The director of the Museum of Modern Art called it "the best family museum I've seen." An editorial in the *St. Louis Post-Dispatch* called it a "sandbox for the inner child . . . where creativity and actual children run wild."

City Museum in downtown St. Louis has been amazing and delighting visitors since it opened in 1997. Housed on the first three floors of the International Arts Complex (formerly the home of the world's largest shoe manufacturer), City Museum takes donations of all kinds and uses imagination to turn them into wonders.

From the top of a giant slide in City Museum, this fantasy world of the imagination looks like the perfect place to live. On one level you can walk (or run) through a 52-foot bowhead whale and emerge onto an observation deck, where you can look into a giant fish tank filled with imaginative sculptures and all sorts of Mississippi River fish. Slip behind the whale and enter dark caves and passages, or walk through the Enchanted Forest and into a giant bird's nest. Exit the nest, if you dare, through an overhead crawl-through tube ending on a castle rooftop.

The adventures seem endless—and dreamlike. Step inside a tidal cave and stand atop boulders as waves crash. Watch a generator from what was once the world's largest windmill power a Rube Goldberg–type contraption that hoists a 24,000-pound block of granite up

You can get swallowed up by City Museum's 4,000 feet of caves.
CITY MUSEUM

and down two stories inside the museum. Join the Everydaycircus and visit a carnival-like midway. Watch artists and crafters practicing their trades, and try your hand at a few yourself.

You can't possibly do it all in a single visit, and before you can get back, some of the temporary exhibits will have changed. But City Museum's mission statement remains: "We believe all people are innately creative and artistic. Our goal is to reawaken the childlike imagination, joy, and sense of wonder in all of us, transforming the way we look at the world."

The museum, located at 701 North Fifteenth Street in downtown St. Louis, is open Wednesday through Sunday in winter; seven days a week in summer (hours vary). Call (314) 231-CITY (2489) or visit www.citymuseum.org for details. Admission charged, with group rates; "free if you are under 2 or over 100." But don't wait for that Super Senior Discount; the museum's well worth the price of admission.

Longest Walk over Water

Built in 1927, the Chain of Rocks Bridge was the first bridge to span the Mississippi River between Missouri and Illinois. Once part of historic Route 66, the bridge has been retired from automobile use and dedicated to pedestrian and bicycle traffic. At 24 feet wide and 5,353 feet long, the Chain of Rocks Bridge is the longest pedestrian bridge in the world. Look for it 12 miles north of the Gateway Arch. Wear comfortable shoes—it's a long way across.

Going to the Dogs

St. Louis

A lot of people really do look like their dogs. Or is it that a lot of dogs really look like their people?

Anyway, the best place to check out the truth of this conventional wisdom is the American Kennel Club Museum of the Dog. Located in the pastoral setting of lovely Queeny Park on the west side of St.

Rin Tin Tin is only one of the gorgeous movie stars featured on the Museum of the Dog's Wall of Fame.
AKC MUSEUM OF THE DOG

Louis, the museum is open year-round for dog lovers, dogs themselves, and even people who just want to look at dogs. Some of the best artwork in the world featuring dogs is on display in the museum's permanent collection and special exhibits.

The 14,000-square-foot facility includes historic Jarville House, built in 1853. It contains more than 500 original paintings, drawings, watercolors, prints, sculptures, and a variety of decorative arts, all depicting dogs. The dog-themed gift shop sells everything imaginable, including jeweled dog dishes and "whine coolers" sporting favorite breeds of woofers. The museum has an extensive book and video library, available by appointment for research on purebred dogs and animal artists. There are also Guest Dog of the Week events and many educational programs throughout the year.

Be sure to check out the AKC Hall of Fame, which each year inducts new honorees in several categories, displaying their images on walls dedicated to America's most remarkable dogs. Lassie is there, with Toto, Rin Tin Tin, and plenty of other pups you'll recognize. This is the only museum I've ever been in where people were walking around with their dogs—inside. I saw jowly, square-jawed men escorting bulldogs. Pretty women with pouffy hair paraded with equally pouffed poodles and Pekingese. Athletic men and women stretched outside and prepared to run on the adjoining trails of Queeny Park with their long-legged, muscular dogs. From what I could see, even mutts and their masters were made welcome. It's not their fault that they don't have a long name and a pedigree.

The museum is located at 1721 South Mason Road. From I-64/US 40 west of St. Louis, take the Mason Road exit; or take the Manchester exit off I-270 to Mason Road. Closed Monday and holidays. Admission charged; memberships available. Call (314) 821-3647 for details.

My, What Big Teeth You Have!
St. Louis

Nobody I know looks forward to a trip to the dentist, but everybody—except, perhaps, Mr. Tooth Decay—will enjoy a trip to Dental Health Theatre. There you can watch movies, see a marionette show, and view exhibits, all of which drill into visitors the golden rules of dental health: brushing, flossing, eating nutritious foods, and visiting the dentist twice a year.

Tackling tartar at the Dental Health Theatre.
DENTAL HEALTH THEATRE

★ ★

Children particularly love the hands-on exhibits, which can help them overcome their fears of their own dental appointments. And as far as being nagged to brush their teeth, what child can complain about brushing their tiny teeth after they have personally brushed the set of sixteen 3-foot-tall fiberglass choppers (that light up) on display here?

You'll find the theater at 727 North First Street at Laclede's Landing, near the Arch. Open year-round Tuesday through Saturday, 9:00 a.m. to 3:00 p.m. A small admission is charged, but they recommend that you call (314) 241-7391 for a reservation.

Mystery Meat, Served with a Side of Laughter
St. Louis

There's a place in St. Louis where you can get a look inside the city's oldest home while having a delicious meal and at the same time watching what some have called "the best whodunit in the country." Only trouble is, somebody isn't coming out alive.

The place is the Bissell Mansion, a mid-1820s home built by a military officer. The mansion still contains many of the original features, which have been preserved through successive renovations. You can choose your meal from among four delicious entrees prepared by an expert staff. The whodunit is any one of several themed comic murder mysteries presented throughout the year.

Guests receive an identity when they arrive, complete with a few facts they are asked to reveal at appropriate moments. Costumes may be arranged beforehand, but you can also come as you are and the staff will see to it that you get enough costume accessories and accouterments to help you play your part with panache.

Everyone is in for a surprise, because the murderer and suspects are selected randomly from the audience, and variables ensure that the script will never play out exactly the same way twice. Guests can indicate what level of participation they prefer, so shy persons need not get indigestion from a bout of stage fright.

Going— and Staying— in Style

In the latter half of the 1800s, Jessie Arnot was the St. Louis livery stable owner you got to take you to the cemetery for the last time, if you really wanted to go in style. He was the only person in the Midwest with a four-horse hearse. As a result, Arnot was the man chosen to transport the body of President Abraham Lincoln from the funeral train at the station to his grave in Springfield, Illinois.

Arnot always knotted his reins so that he could control his four-horse team with one hand, and he used to tie his necktie with the same unique signature knot. Lots of us guys still use the "four-in-hand" when someone makes us wear a tie. Jessie's own grave is in Bellefontaine Cemetery, St. Louis.

But beware! Some ingenues have agreed to go out and play what they thought was a mere suspicious character but come back a murderous star.

Regular performances are Friday and Saturday nights, plus there is a Sunday matinee. Any number of guests are welcome to join the fun with advance reservations. Special weeknights and matinees may be scheduled for groups of at least thirty people; discounts for regular performances are available for groups of as few as ten.

Bissell Mansion Restaurant & Murder Mystery Dinner Theatre is located at 4426 Randall Place. For information call (800) 690-9838 or visit www.bissellmansiontheatre.com.

Fertile Ground

Would-be songwriters would do well to study the biographies of some of the interesting people interred at St. Peter's Cemetery in St. Louis. Many of them led colorful if controversial lives, and their stories are the stuff of immortality.

Take William "Willie" Lyons, who was shot and killed by his friend Lee Shelton on Christmas Eve 1885. The two good buddies got into an argument, fueled by alcohol, at a saloon on the corner of Eleventh and Morgan (now Delmar). This tragedy got translated into the song "Stagger Lee," which can be found on many honky-tonk jukeboxes today.

Another hapless victim whose sad fate has been set to famous verse is Allen Britt, who was fatally shot October 15, 1899, by his girlfriend, Miss Frankie Baker, a reputed "red light" girl. This tale of woe became the subject of the song "Frankie and Albert" (a slight change from "Al Britt"), but that didn't have quite the right ring to it, so the name was changed to "Frankie and Johnny." Like so many other songs of reckless love, it became a huge hit, recorded since by countless singers and even turned into a movie.

Not all the musical celebrities in St. Peter's Cemetery are versified victims, however. Also check out the grave of ragtime pianist and composer Thomas M. J. Turpin (1871–1922), whose notable hits include "Ta-Ra-Ra-Boom-De-Ay" and "Hot Time in the Old Town Tonight."

Rooms without a View

St. Louis

If you are not from St. Louis—and maybe even if you are—when you drive by Fourteenth Street and US 40, you may be fooled by a beautiful building with lots of windows. Now the Sheraton City Center Hotel, the facade of the landmark Edison Brothers Warehouse built in 1929 features a trompe l'oeil mural of scenes from the 1904 World's Fair. Those windows and ledges aren't real; they are just painted on.

The lifelike facade is a foil for pigeons.

★ ★

When the Sheraton Corporation purchased the locally famous warehouse, renovation efforts went to removing a central portion of eight floors to create the largest atrium in Missouri, encompassing more than 1.2 million cubic feet from the fifth to the thirteenth floors. Hotel rooms, suites, and condominiums wrap around the atrium, giving them a wonderful interior view.

Which is great, because this allowed the architects to preserve the amazing, antique optical illusion on the exterior walls. I had been told it was there ahead of time, and I had to look twice to make sure I was looking at the right building and not one with real windows. I felt better when, as I was taking a photograph, I saw a pigeon fly up and try to land on one of the painted-on ledges. Boy, was he surprised. Not even Spider-Man could get a toehold on that sheer wall.

The building is located at 400 South Fourteenth Street. Call (314) 231-5007 for more information.

Strings Attached
St. Louis

In an era of electronic toys and video games, Bob Kramer's Marionnette Theater is an old-fashioned delight. Founded in 1963, Kramer's Theater doesn't just entertain. As part of their mission, staff members also conduct demonstrations that educate children and adults to the history of this centuries-old but nearly lost art form and the manner in which puppeteers transform limp cloth and cold hardwood into characters that are breathtakingly lifelike.

Bob Kramer and his partner, Dug Feltch, have taken their troupe of marionettes all over the world. In the United States their work is recognized for such whimsical creations as the 4-foot spider that sat atop the Hallmark float in the Macy's Thanksgiving Day Parade and such educational aids as the 7-foot baby dinosaur that appeared with Marlin Perkins at the St. Louis Science Center. Another favorite creation is Bone A Part, the 9-foot dog. Something magical happens when a marionette raises her head or lifts his arm in a lifelike gesture.

Where President Dubb-ya Got It

First came President George Herbert Walker Bush, and then later we got President George W. Bush. This is going to give schoolchildren at least as much confusion as that John Adams–John Quincy Adams thing.

George Walker Bush isn't a junior; he doesn't have the Herbert in there. Since childhood people have distinguished the son from his dad by calling him just "George W." or, in Texas-speak, simply "Dubb-ya."

Ever wondered where that "W" came from? Before it was his, and before his dad even had one, the great-great-grandfather of Dubb-ya was one—a Walker, that is. David Davis Walker, great-great-grandfather of George W. Bush, put the Walker family on the map and in the chips when he founded the Eli Walker Company, a dry goods wholesale company based in St. Louis.

If you want to see something of the Walker who lent his name to two American presidents, you can visit his gravesite in Calvary Cemetery, on West Florissant Avenue near the Broadway exit off I-70 in St. Louis.

Children who are painfully shy with other people sometimes open up and communicate freely with puppets, even though they can see the strings or hear the puppeteer throw his voice.

A cast of more than 800 puppets waits for the call to entertain you daily at Bob Kramer's Marionnette Theater, located at 4143 Laclede Avenue, Laclede's Landing. Call (314) 531-3313 for show and demonstration times, or visit www.kramersmarionnettes.com.

Towering above Us

At the intersection of Twentieth Street and East Grand Avenue in St. Louis stands a lonely white 154-foot Corinthian column. Many people think the building it came from must have been enormous. But the truth is the Grand ("Old White") Tower isn't really a column, and it never was used to support a building.

Old White is an obsolete water tower, one of only seven so-called "standpipe" water towers remaining in the United States. Once hundreds of standpipes could be found all over the country. St. Louis has three of the seven that remain; another, the minaret-like 194-foot Bissell, is visible just a few blocks away at the intersection of Blair and Bissell.

Standpipes were not water reservoirs, as we think of water towers today; rather they were large vertical pipes in which water levels rose and fell to equalize water pressure and prevent surges caused by the powerful steam-driven water pumps used in the nineteenth and early twentieth centuries. In more affluent communities, standpipes were surrounded by decorative towers for aesthetic reasons.

Old White was completed in 1871, during the tenure of waterworks director Thomas J. Whitman (brother to famous poet, Walt), and served until it was retired in 1912. Designed by architect George I. Barnett at a cost of $45,000, the brick tower rests on an octagonal base of Chicago stone and is topped by a cast-iron capital in a leaf design. Lights placed atop the tower in the 1920s were used as navigational aids by pilots flying into Lambert Field. Supposedly they once helped Charles Lindbergh land safely when he was lost in a Mississippi River fog.

Efforts to dismantle the neighboring Old White and Bissell Towers were thwarted in 1933 and 1958, respectively, and they remain as curious landmarks today. Their younger cousin standpipe, the 179-foot Compton Hill Tower, across town at Compton Heights, is even more elaborate and still contains a stairway that is occasionally opened to the public for panoramic viewing of the city skyline. While this tower both startles and amuses some people with its bold, masculine, and less-than-subtle styling, a nearby statue of *The Naked Truth*, a female nude, manages to divert the public's attention.

People figure St. Louis really used to build 'em big when they catch a glimpse of Old White.

★ ★

The World's First Airmail

St. Louis

A lot of brouhaha is made over the Pony Express and how fast those riders on horseback could deliver the mail. But the fact is, a much faster, airmail delivery was launched from Washington Square in St. Louis on July 1, 1859—a year before the Pony Express came into its short existence.

The French like to claim that they came up with the idea for airmail when in 1870 an attempt was made to send messages over enemy lines in a balloon launched from Paris. But eleven years earlier, there was mail aboard an experimental flight from Missouri to New York piloted by aeronaut John Wise, with scientist O. A. Gager, balloon builder John LaMountain, and newspaperman William Hyde aboard. The men were testing Gager's theory that Earth's rotation caused prevailing east–west air currents.

Like other balloons of the time, which were primarily used as attractions at circuses and fairs, the historic craft was made of varnished Chinese silk, with a basket beneath. In case touchdown had to be made on water, a boat was suspended below the basket that held the passengers.

Taking off from St. Louis after 7:00 p.m., the crew reached an estimated altitude of 2 miles in the darkness. When they awoke, ice had formed on their water buckets and LaMountain was bleeding from his nose. Below them was Lake Erie. They quickly released gas and descended. The men were astonished to realize how fast they had traveled when, by the middle of the day, they heard the roar of Niagara Falls. Passing over the falls, they were nearly lost in a violent storm over Lake Ontario.

To regain altitude, the four cast off all the ballast they could, including their boat, which probably would not have stayed afloat in the violent waters anyway. The balloon bounced on the water four times but finally carried them over land again. They were prevented from making a controlled landing because the balloon's valve had become frozen. Strong winds blew them into a forest, and they only managed to avoid being thrown out when the balloon punctured by hanging onto the steel ring that attached the balloon to the basket. Shaken but uninjured, the men climbed down from the treetops near Henderson, New York, almost 1,000 miles from St. Louis. The trip had taken them just over nineteen hours.

And what about the mail? That had been some of the ballast cast off over Lake Ontario, but it was found and delivered, thus completing the first piloted airmail service in history.

This New House
St. Louis

Forget all your notions that old houses have to be drafty and uncomfortable. Back in 1994 the Missouri Botanical Garden took an 1885 Victorian home suffering from severe neglect and with modern technology transformed it into the EarthWays Center, an environmentally friendly house the most sophisticated techno-wonk would love. A tour of it is like a journey into the future.

Features of the house include clever low-wattage lighting sources, the most modern recycled and nontoxic products on the market, water-saving devices, recycling and composting equipment, a variety of energy-efficient window options, a photovoltaic solar system powering the house's high-efficiency kitchen appliances, a geothermal heating and cooling system, a high-efficiency gas furnace, and efficient landscaping. Everywhere you turn you get ideas of what could make your life and home easier, less expensive, and environmentally responsible.

The EarthWays Center gives workshops throughout the year that focus on environmentally friendly practices, and in summer they hold Camp EarthWays, which finds fun ways to teach environmentalism to children.

The worm composting system for dealing with the home's garbage is one of the most popular aspects of the house, especially for kids. Eco-celebrities such as Mary Appelhof, the self-described "Worm Woman," have made appearances at the EarthWays Center to generate interest in environmental concerns and practices.

The EarthWays Center is located at 3617 Grandel Square. Public tours are given for a small fee on the third Saturday and Sunday of each month. Group tours can be arranged by appointment at other times. For more information call (314) 577-0220 or visit www.earthwayscenter.org.

The Worm Woman wiggled her way into the hearts of visitors.
MARY FRANCIS FENTON, FLOWERFIELD ENTERPRISES

Hold That Tiger!

Ste. Genevieve

If any other owner of a bed-and-breakfast establishment told me to "leave your cares at the gate" and enjoy the "peaceful retreat," I would have an easier time complying than I do when I read the same words in Joe Scott's brochure for Crown Ridge lodge and restaurant.

You see, Crown Ridge is not just a three-bedroom lodge; it's also a tiger sanctuary. Gates here are not just for ornamentation. When I picture myself in a retreat at Crown Ridge, I don't see myself at peace. It's more like a mad dash.

Crown Ridge Tiger Sanctuary was created a few years ago by a couple in association with DePaul University. They had rescued a litter of five cubs born in captivity to a white tiger (one in the litter is white too), and with that success they imagined they could provide a home and research center for other domesticated big cats that would be hopelessly unfit for life in the wild. Subsequently, officials at DePaul decided to sell the property, which was then bought by Scott.

Scott owns the neighboring 8,000-acre Crown Valley Winery, which perfectly complements the scale of a lodge and restaurant. For about $200 a night you can lie in one of the lodge's claw-foot beds and drift off to sleep wondering what that noise you just heard was.

Security is well thought out for visitors and tigers alike. Viewings of the tigers can be arranged outside double fencing, just outside the inner fence, or from a tree house in the huge enclosed tiger grounds.

In addition to the meals prepared for guests of the lodge, the chef prepares theme dinners, including French Provençal, Italian, St. Patrick's Day, Easter, and Mother's Day.

If your mother-in-law has never liked you and always seems dissatisfied with everything you do, maybe you should take her to Crown Royal for dinner—and the optional tour where visitors feed the tigers.

For information and directions call (573) 833-9909 or visit www.crown-ridge.com.

★ ★

Planning Ahead

Writers often have this thing about getting their epitaphs right. One way to ensure success is to have your tombstone inscribed and planted on your plot *before* you cross over. James R. Peters, who writes under the pen names of George L. Bond and George Gray, has done this for himself at his intended resting place in the Iona Cemetery in Cape Girardeau County. Quoting from Peters's gravestone, which indicates that he was born in 1946 but has not died yet:

I WARNED YOU THIS WOULD HAPPEN,

TOO MUCH INFO HE HAS READ

TOO MUCH INFO IN HIS HEAD

TOO MUCH INFO—NOW HE'S DEAD.

Let's just hope the clever and witty Mr. Peters still has a lot to learn.

Hurling Hot Ones

Sikeston

People might sling hash to customers in some joints or toss food onto the tables for the clientele in others, but I guarantee you that Lambert's is the only place you're gonna eat Throwed Rolls. Throwed Rolls are a trademark food item of Lambert's Cafe, and nobody can pitch one over your plate better.

Lambert's Cafe was started in 1942 by Earl and Agnes Lambert. With only 14 cents between them, the couple borrowed $1,500 and opened a little restaurant on South Main Street in Sikeston that seated forty-one people—if everybody got along. Wartime rationing called for creative cooking, especially on meatless days, but the Lamberts made it work and developed a small following.

Earl Lambert died in 1976, and Agnes sold the place. But her son, Norman, bought it back a week later and joined his mom in the business. When, after forty years, the old place "simply wore out," the Lamberts moved to another location on East Malone that was three times as big. Quality food, served in ample quantities to people who were treated as guests instead of customers, proved to be a formula for success. Crowds began standing in line to get into Lambert's.

Norman, who had been a shy man, learned to overcome his shyness and began to joke with his guests. He even had a few magic tricks he would perform for them. One day when the place was really hopping, Norm couldn't get around people to serve a customer another roll he wanted. Finally the man shouted, "Just throw the #@%$ thing," so Norm did—to considerable applause—and a trademark was born.

People loved to go to Lambert's Cafe for the good food, friendly atmosphere, and the silly thrill of having a server pitch them a hot roll. Seven years later the Lamberts had outgrown their second location, so they opened a place that would seat 300 out on the edge of town. By then Norm's basic philosophies had become "13 Golden Rules" stressing satisfaction and quality, over and over again.

Norm would tell people in wheelchairs, "You brought your own chair, so you can eat free." He gave away uncounted Christmas dinners. Above all, with the help of his family and staff, Norman Lambert delighted his guests. Norman has since died, as did his cherished son, Todd, but the family institution he created is alive and well.

Crowds still line up outside Lambert's Cafe to become guests. (Two more Lambert's have opened—in Ozark, Missouri, and Foley, Alabama.) Once inside, you order your main course and a team of fresh-faced, cheerful servers comes around with friendly banter and endless helpings of free "pass-arounds." The tasty fried potatoes and onions, macaroni and tomatoes, black-eyed peas, and okra have

★ ★

become so popular that they had to be added as a special menu item for people who didn't want to eat anything else—except, of course, those great, hot homemade rolls that are served only one way.

"Heads up, Lady! Hot roll comin' at ya!"

Lambert's Cafe (573-471-4261) is located at 2305 East Malone in Sikeston (and 1800 West Highway J in Ozark). Check them out at www.throwedrolls.com.

There's only one way to pass the rolls at Lambert's.
MISSOURI DIVISION OF TOURISM

Just Jake
Wardell

Years ago I stopped at a little restaurant in Hayti, outside Caruthersville, for breakfast. When I mentioned that I was a writer looking for "people who kinda color outside the lines," the two waitresses, the cook, and the girl busing tables all looked at each other and said, "Jake."

They directed me about 15 miles up the road to Wardell, where they said I would spot Jake's place by the mannequin outside wearing an American flag minidress and a patriotic hard hat. One of the waitresses told me I should describe Wardell as "a town so flat you can sit on your porch and watch your dog run away for three days." Her metaphor is apt.

I found Jake's mannequin with no problem (Wardell is as small as it is flat), but I found no sign of Jake. Well, I can't exactly say that, because parked out front of Jake's place was his little Rampage truck, with a neon sign in the window that read JAKE. Through the screen door I could see lots more neon signs, a bunch of old movie posters, and a monkey bike with tiny tires, just like circus clowns ride.

The post office was just two doors down, so I stopped and asked about Jake. The postmaster sent me to a convenience store being built at the other end of the block, which he said was one of Jake's entrepreneurial ventures. But I didn't find Jake at that ghostlike worksite, either. Soon, however, Jake appeared from parts unknown, driving a turquoise Festiva. He apologized for driving such an unnecessarily large vehicle around town, explaining that he normally rode his reproduction Whizzer motorbike.

The first business card Jake handed me gave his (a)vocations as "International Playboy & Private Investigator." His motto proclaimed, "Call me . . . I will look into anything!" This would not seem terribly difficult in a town as small as Wardell, but Jake's card gave a second address of Melbourne, Australia. Later in our conversation I learned that Jake had, indeed, lived and worked for a time in the oil industry

Down Under. He told me he still had good contacts there and would
be glad to go back.

Jake humorously dismissed a tour he did in Vietnam, referring to
himself as "a 200 percent disabled Vet." He still had contacts there
too. Jake operated another business—locating used draglines, which
are bought by companies draining parts of Southeast Asia, the way
southeast Missouri was drained years ago. Jake handed me another
business card, advertising, "Draglines Wanted, Dead or Alive." This
card had just Jake's American phone numbers and an e-mail address.
When he mentioned a Missouri magazine where he advertised to find
old draglines, I realized that I had seen his ads without realizing such
a colorful character had placed them.

But there was little else about Jake I had seen anywhere before.
His "place" was at one end of the post office/movie theater/Rex-
alls Drugstore that used to serve as a town hub; Jake had inherited
it from a relative. The theater showed its last film about 1957 and
looked like Godzilla just stormed out, but Jake told me he was working on a renovation plan. The old Rexalls had become Jake's shop,
workroom, and office, with an apartment in the back. A few years
previously Jake had a health scare that caused him to put his affairs
in order, at which time he sold the post office end of his building. His
health later improved, and he said he missed the extra income.

The convenience store he was building on the corner was another
part of Jake's Wardell renewal plan, since the town no longer had a
place to buy gasoline. Kind of like a one-man chamber of commerce,
Jake had a sense of history and a notion of where the town needed
to go to get back on track.

Wardell was once the smallest town in the United States with a
Lion's Club. The drainage ditch across from Jake's place used to be
navigable by small boats all the way to the Mississippi River. Clint
Walker's dad used to have a sawmill in Wardell, and the cowboy
movie and TV star would show up in town from time to time.

But Jake never wasted time thinking of the old days. A compulsive

Jake of Wardell with the model he shopped for and the
prototype of his one-day world-famous airbike.

inventor, one day he slapped a Zinger airplane propeller onto a
Weedeater motor and attached the whole thing to an old English
bike. He and a friend got his airbike up to 39 miles an hour before he
decided he should make some modifications. Better brakes came to
my mind.

A huge fan of both the Little Rascals and Eddie Murphy, Jake
also invented what he called "the OTAY meter," a giant neon sign
hooked up to a motion sensor and a bell. Every time somebody
approached Jake's house, the bell went off and the sign flashed OTAY,

★ ★

expressing Jake's general attitude, as well as his love of visitors.

Sadly Jake passed away in 2008. I used to say that if you were driving anywhere near the Wardells (there's a North Wardell too), I would recommend dropping by to see how Jake Fisher was coming along with his various projects. Nowadays I suggest that if you find yourself in Wardell, ask the locals what they remember about my old friend Jake. Like a stray sunflower popping up and blooming brightly all by itself in the middle of a boring field of soybeans, Jake made people smile. Just talking to Jake was a trip way past Wardell. I hope his memory will inspire people for a long time to come.

Wardell is on State Route A, west of I-55 and north of Caruthersville.

Smoke 'Em If You've Got 'Em
Washington

Even nonsmokers will enjoy a tour of the Corn Cob Pipe Museum in Washington, the "Corn Cob Capital of the World." At one time there were a dozen or more companies in the community cranking out corncob pipes, but only the original Missouri Meerschaum Company remains.

Plenty of farmers used to use quickly carved corncob pipes to smoke homegrown tobacco back in the nineteenth century. Corncob pipes and hillbillies were synonymous. But nobody would have thought to buy one.

Then, about the time of the Civil War, a man asked Dutch-born woodworker Henry Tibbe to turn a pipe bowl out of a corncob on his wood lathe. Tibbe made a few extra and placed them in the window of his shop, where they quickly sold.

Tibbe worked with a chemist to devise a plaster-based substance to coat the lathe-turned corncob pipe bowls, and in 1878 he was granted a patent for the process. The inexpensive pipes are said to rival the extraordinary properties of the genuine porous Turkish clay meerschaum (meaning "sea foam") pipes, preferred by smokers for their cool draw. Gen. Douglas MacArthur was so associated with his tall corncob pipe that they named the style for him.

Even with a decline in tobacco use, the Missouri Meerschaum Company today produces about 5,000 pipes a day for the worldwide market. Tours of the factory are not given, but the associated Corn Cob Pipe Museum next door is a great place to learn fun facts about these ingenious pipes. For example, while most farmers were trying to grow corn with smaller cobs, the University of Missouri was asked to develop a strain with larger cobs, better suited to pipe making. The Missouri Meerschaum Company has about 150 acres of that specialized corn in production, and some years they pay farmers to grow even more. Modern shelling equipment pulverizes the cobs, so the corn is removed from pipe cobs using antique shelling equipment.

The Corn Cob Pipe Museum is located at 400 Front Street, at the corner of Front and Cedar, one block from the Amtrak station. The museum is open Monday through Friday from 8:00 a.m. to 3:30 p.m. Call (636) 239-2109 or (800) 888-2109 or visit www.corncobpipe.com for more information.

A Super Site to Hike or Bike

Weldon Spring

This has got to be the quintessential example of turning lemons into lemonade. It also might qualify as one of the most bizarre ecotourism adventures you'll ever take.

The Nuclear Waste Adventure Trail and Museum in Weldon Spring sit atop a Super Fund cleanup site where for decades the government manufactured explosives; products containing arsenic, lead, and asbestos; plus enriched uranium for nuclear weapons. Now you can go there to hike, bike, and ponder America's nuclear program during the cold war.

★ ★

Originally a site where the army manufactured TNT, the facility was turned over to the Atomic Energy Commission (now the Department of Energy, or DOE) in 1955 for uranium processing, while chemical and conventional weapons continued to be produced there.

When the plant was finally shut down in the 1980s and the magnitude of the waste problem became clear, the DOE spent almost $1 billion to clean up the site. A forty-five–acre "waste tomb" disposal cell made of stone, concrete, and clay covers the processed debris and rises seven stories over the surrounding countryside. On a clear day you can see St. Louis and the Gateway Arch 35 miles to the east.

Visitors can walk or bike the 6-mile Adventure Trail, which is dotted with plaques describing the site's history and bits of America's cold war history. The building that formerly housed a radioactive worker detection checkpoint has been converted to an interpretive center museum where you can learn more fun or chilling facts, depending on your point of view.

The site also includes a lovely eight-acre native plant display and the adjoining 150-acre Howell Prairie. The 10-mile Hamburg Trail traverses the entire area, providing recreation to hikers and bikers. Hamburg and Howell were two villages displaced by the weapons plant in World War II.

When the Nuclear Waste Adventure Trail and Museum were opened, a project manager for the DOE stated, "You don't tell people they're safe by putting fences around something. Fences communicate a very negative barrier."

To commune with nature at Weldon Spring and see how well you think the government has done its job, take MO 94 south from I-70, west of St. Louis. Open during daylight hours; admission is free (if you don't count the $1 billion). For more information visit www.wssrap.com.

Walking (or Riding) the Plank

Due to the unbelievable abundance of timber and the scarcity of decent roads, in 1851 the Missouri legislature authorized the building of plank, or so-called "corduroy," roads. These were privately financed highways; investors were supposed to recoup their investment and receive handsome profits by charging tolls. The only trouble was, plank roads were a splintering failure.

A total of seventeen such roads were actually built, and within twenty years almost all of them went bankrupt. The longest plank road actually completed ran approximately 50 miles from Ste. Genevieve to Iron Mountain via Farmington (a route now largely supplanted by MO 32).

The law stated that plank roads must be at least 50 feet wide, with wooden planks at the center and the remainder of the road composed of dirt, gravel, or macadam. Wood road centers averaged 8 to 12 feet wide, but winters were hard on the timbers, leaving them alternately heaved or sunken by the constant pressures of freezing and thawing. Heavy rains also undermined the success of plank roads.

Owners were authorized to prevent passage by travelers until tolls were paid, with the stipulation that pedestrians, suckling cows, and suckling horses could travel free. Tollbooth operators were also prevented from detaining travelers for an "unreasonable" period of time. Remember that the next time you are stuck in traffic.

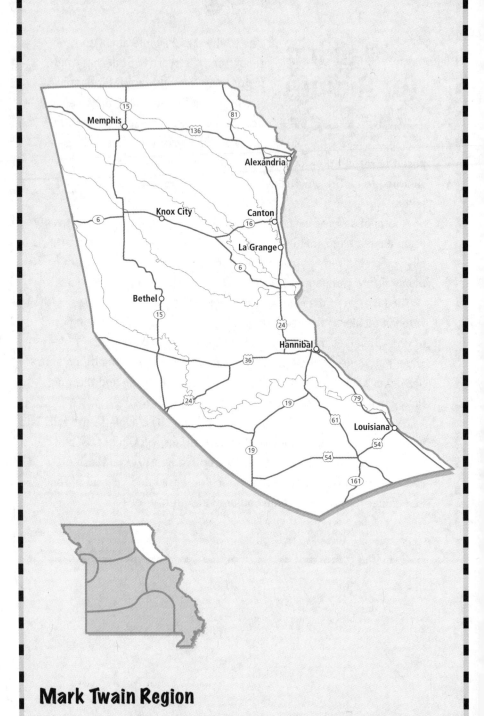

Mark Twain Region

2

Mark Twain Region

The ten counties in extreme northeast Missouri still bask in the glow of Samuel Langhorne Clemens's literary fame nearly a hundred years after his death. River trade no longer dominates these small, scattered farming communities the way it once did, but people who live there seem to believe that when Mark Twain wrote about simpler times and colorful childhood adventures, he was writing about them. In nearly all of Mark Twain's writings, there are also strange, bizarre, and usually funny people, places, and things just outside the main plot. Northeast Missouri is like that.

On the surface the region seems placid, like the Mississippi on a calm summer day. But if travelers take a plunge and venture deeper, they may discover surprising treasures and dark secrets. Here you will find marvelous architecture from a bygone age in towns that can no longer support a grocery store or a bank. This makes northeast Missouri an antiques lover's paradise, as people who now occupy once stately homes and businesses empty them of forgotten contents and one-of-a-kind items that may not match a modern remodeler's plans. Fortunes were made here long ago, and people used their wealth to travel widely and educate their children well. Items you might watch for in this unexpected locale include rare books, fine art, and cultural artifacts from around the world. Don't think you'll necessarily outsmart every local yokel having a yard sale, though. Some of these crusty old farmers are graduates of Harvard or Yale.

★ ★

Gee, Geodes!
Alexandria

For almost fifty years, just south of the Iowa state line, where US 136 met US 61 north of Alexandria, there was a little hidden treasure. The Sheffler Rock Shop and Geode Mine was founded in the late 1950s by "the Geode Lady," Betty Sheffler. Originally she ran the operation from her kitchen counter. Now Betty's son, Tim, runs things, but people still want to talk geodes with Betty.

Geodes are lumpy round rocks that look pretty boring on the outside but when split open reveal a wonderment of dazzling quartz crystals. Sheffler geodes are prized among rock hounds, who recognize their rare gem-quality quartz. Ferdinand Marcos used to order Sheffler geodes to decorate his presidential palace in the Philippines.

Be prepared for hard, dirty work if you want to dig your own geodes. For $25 per person you can take your own picks and shovels (plus hammers, chisels, sledges, and pry bars) into the Sheffler mines, which are basically creekbeds, and dig out up to fifty pounds of rocky plunder. Some people whack their geodes open then and there, but real experts wait to cut them open with proper tools at home. You can tell a good, potentially show-quality geode by its light weight, which indicates a large hollow space inside.

If you are lazy, or don't want to break a fingernail, you can buy geodes out of the shop without getting your hands dirty or your muscles sore. Prices average a few dollars for small ones to $40 and more for large, choice geodes. Tim has also added fossils and other rocks of interest from elsewhere.

The old Sheffler Rock Shop sadly was displaced by a highway project, the so-called "Avenue of the Saints," which runs from St. Paul, Minnesota, to St. Louis. It seems a shame that something called the Avenue of the Saints wiped out a place where people went in search of one of God's rare and beautiful creations. Betty and Tim fortunately managed to relocate nearby. With Tim's help, customers can still mine the same magical ground.

Mining season is generally April through December, plus whatever warm spells allow the Shefflers to open in winter. The new Sheffler Rock Shop is located 2.5 miles south of Wayland (take the Keokuk exit off US 61 and MO 27). For more information call (660) 754-1134 or visit http://homepages.vvm.com/~sheffler.

Counting Sheep

Bethel

The tiny German community town of Bethel has only about one hundred residents, but every Labor Day weekend for nearly a quarter century it has been the location for the World Sheep and Fiber Arts Festival, when 4,000 to 5,000 people happily flock around the hamlet to see sheep such as you may never have seen before. Many rare and exotic breeds are shown, such as the bizarre multihorned Jacob sheep, as well as champion examples of standard varieties.

There are lots of sheep-theme booths where you can buy woolen garments, fleecy finery, sheepish signs, and cute sheep toys. Vendors are there, too, for sheep farmers who want to keep up on the latest equipment to handle their flocks. Succulent sheep snacks scent the air and tempt your taste buds. Whatever your level of interest in the woolly ones, everyone is fascinated by the sheepdog demonstrations. In England the annual sheepdog trials are at the top of the TV ratings. Here is your chance to see the same kind of thing live and up close, complete with smell-o-rama.

Other popular events include the "Fiber to Shawl" competition, where contestants race to see who can produce a finished shawl from wool on the hoof, and a similar race to get from a fleece to any finished article of apparel. There is an annual style show, with models wearing everything from vintage to contemporary design clothing. Or take the kids "Mutton Bustin," a hilarious rodeo romp where they can ride fluffy, bucking baa-baas. If you get tuckered out by all the activities, there are also plenty of places to sit quietly and just start counting sheep. Daily admission rates are very reasonable, and

★ ★

people who are there for all three days can get even cheaper week-end passes.

Bethel is in northern Shelby County, on MO 15 west of Hannibal and Palmyra. For more information call Donnie Parsons, evenings, (573) 439-5035, or visit www.worldsheepfest.com.

Are We Almost There Yet?
Canton

Used to be that people lived for the day bridges would span the Mississippi and make their lives easier. Bridges across the Mississippi at St. Louis and Louisiana, Missouri, were among the first and helped those cities to prosper. Now we treasure the few remaining ferries left. They remind us, if only dimly, of how things used to be.

The Canton Ferry is the longest continually operated ferry service

At Canton the longest continuously operated ferry service on the Mississippi used to be powered by two horses on treadmills.

★ ★

on the Mississippi River. Established about 1844 just north of Canton, the ferry was originally powered by two horses walking on treadmills connected to paddle wheels. Nowadays two 195 horsepower diesel engines chug you across in five or ten minutes.

The first recorded charter for the ferry was issued February 24, 1853, to Christian University (now Culver-Stockton College, but they no longer operate the ferry). Fees then were "Footmen 10¢, Team & Wagon 50¢." Today cars and pickups go one-way for $5, round-trip for $9. If you tell them you are a footman, they'll laugh so hard that you might get across for a dime, but the return trip will probably cost you $8.90.

Take either Canton exit off US 61. You'll drive parallel to the river and can't miss the little park where the ferry is located. The ferry runs Monday through Friday 7:00 a.m. to 7:00 p.m. and Saturday and Sunday 8:00 a.m. to 7:00 p.m., except when conditions are icy. Average time for a crossing is about five minutes.

A Whitewash

Hannibal

Clear back in 1876, Mark Twain gave away the reverse-psychology ruse when he wrote *The Adventures of Tom Sawyer*. Tom, as you may recall, was assigned the onerous chore of whitewashing his Aunt Polly's fence. By pretending to love the job, Tom tricked his friends into lining up to take their turns at relieving him, even bribing him with boyish treasures for just a chance to try their hand at it. Well here we are in the twenty-first century, and children are still lining up for their chance to slap whitewash on a fence where Mark Twain lived when he was just known as little Sam Clemens.

It happens each year during the Fourth of July celebrations called Tom Sawyer Days in Hannibal. There are prizes for costumes as well as fence-painting prowess. By the end of the competition, it is questionable whether the fences or the contestants are covered with more paint.

**The official Tom Sawyers in Hannibal know
how to avoid hard work.**
HANNIBAL CONVENTION AND VISITORS BUREAU

Visitors who have outgrown their desire to whitewash someone else's fence may enjoy playing mud volleyball, shopping at a craft fair, sampling the vittles of various food vendors, or merely wandering about this colorful, historic town.

For more information contact the Hannibal Convention and Visitors Bureau at (573) 221-2477 or visit www.visithannibal.com.

Where She Learned to Stay Afloat
Hannibal

The huge popularity of the movie *Titanic* brought the memory of one of its most famous and flamboyant passengers bobbing back up. The self-proclaimed "Unsinkable Molly Brown" survived the maritime disaster with characteristic bravery and quick thinking.

Born in the Mississippi River town of Hannibal to poor Irish immigrants, Molly lived and worked here until she was eighteen years old. Following her father to the Colorado mine fields, she married J. J. Brown, a struggling mining engineer. Her husband's development of a method for using straw bales to support deeper mining made possible the world's greatest gold strike up to that time. When J. J. received a one-eighth share in the "Little Jonny" mine, the Browns were suddenly millionaires, rich beyond belief.

Molly used her newfound wealth to become quite well educated and to buy her way into Denver society. She championed a number of social and humanitarian causes and became an insatiable world traveler.

Thus it was that Molly found herself in Europe when a family health crisis caused her to book last-minute passage on the ill-fated ship in order to return to her hometown of Hannibal. No other family members were with her, but she was traveling with her friends, John Jacob Astor and his young second wife. When the *Titanic* struck the iceberg, Molly was thrown out of bed by the impact, but she had the presence of mind to dress in many layers of clothing and tuck $500 safely in a pocket.

She did not immediately seek a place for herself on a lifeboat but instead tried to calm passengers (particularly the immigrants from steerage) and to help others find exits for escape. She found herself thrown against her will into a lifeboat launched prematurely by the crewman aboard, who wisely directed the passengers to row away from the sinking ship to avoid being pulled under when it went down. Afterward he refused to allow the other passengers to return to look for survivors, upsetting Molly greatly.

Molly shared her extra layers of clothing and organized the women to take their turns at rowing so that they all might stay warm. When they were finally rescued, she used her fluency in five foreign languages to organize and comfort the immigrant survivors, and she contributed her $500 of emergency cash to start a fund for

No Help to Riverboat Pilots

The Mark Twain Memorial Lighthouse, built on Cardiff Hill above Hannibal to celebrate the one-hundredth anniversary of Samuel Clemens's birth, has never been used for navigation, even though it overlooks the Mississippi River. President Franklin Roosevelt first turned it on via telegraph lines in 1935, and it has been rededicated by Presidents Kennedy and Clinton. But it has never functioned as a real lighthouse.

The lady who had it built to honor Mark Twain apparently thought it would be nice to light the way for riverboat captains. But apparently they were more concerned about watching for snags in the river and had no use for a beacon up on the hill.

Mark Twain would see the humor in that.

Built on More Solid Ground

Hannibal was established on land first deeded to Abraham Bird—through an earthquake certificate. Bird was a farmer near New Madrid in 1811, when the infamous earthquake struck. His land was "swallowed up" when the earth opened and the Mississippi River changed its course. Earthquake certificates issued by the federal government entitled those who lost land to have other property in Missouri.

destitute victims. Through her efforts more than $10,000 was raised among the surviving first-class passengers. For the rest of her life, Molly Brown continued her outspoken good works, finally exhausting her fortune at the time of her death with a donation to benefit miners' children.

You can visit this extraordinary woman's birthplace and the museum dedicated to her memory at 600 Butler Avenue, at the junction of US 36 and Denkler's Alley. Open daily June through August; weekends only in April, May, September, and October. Admission is charged. For more information call (573) 221-2100 or visit www.visit mollybrown.com.

A Morel Man
Knox City

As you are driving through Knox City on MO 6, you can't miss Bobby Goodwin's big morels on the north side of the highway, by the park. Where I live, morel mushrooms are just a few inches tall and usually disappear if you don't pick them in about three or four days. The biggest one Bobby's got is 15 feet, 6 inches tall, and it's been there for more than three years.

The north Missouri farmer has 160 acres outside town where he plants row crops, usually rotating soybeans and wheat. In his spare time he makes log letter signs to sell, and sometimes give away. (The big sign that reads KNOX CITY PARK is one of his.)

One day Bobby got looking at a big ole elm on his farm, and he began to see a morel in it. (This is appropriate, as morels often spring up under elms in the springtime.) Being an independent fellow, Bobby laid a couple of telephone poles down and cut the elm so that it would drop onto the poles. That way, he proudly told me, once he limbed the tree, he could use a cane hook to turn the elm tree as he carved it into the shape of a giant wild mushroom. A buddy who uses a cherry picker for handling lumber logs helped Bobby set the mushroom upright in his yard, where it sits, flat on the ground, without anchoring.

Goodwin says folks are welcome to stop and take pictures anytime they want, but on an extremely windy day, I'd still recommend that you stand back and use your telephoto lens. Even if one of his medium-size morels blows over on you, you'll be mush.

Trivia

Mark Twain and Molly Brown are but two of many famous people who were born and/or raised in Hannibal. Another was William P. Lear, inventor of the car radio, the automatic pilot, and the Learjet. Cliff Edwards was also born in Hannibal; you know him better as the voice of Jiminy Cricket in Walt Disney's *Pinocchio*

In Knox City they harvest morels with a chain saw.

Catch as Catch Can

La Grange

In the early years of the twenty-first century, Missouri participated in a great experiment. Joining several Southern states (and doing what quite a few good ole boys have been doing whether it was legal or not), the Show Me State briefly legalized noodling.

Hand fishing is what it stated on the $7 permits, but noodling is noodling. This fishing sport happens when a fella strips off all but the clothes he absolutely needs, then wallers along the banks of a stream reaching into holes and under logs until he finds a catfish nest. Then he grabs the fish by the jaw or the gills and attempts to land it using only his strength and cunning. How a person willing to do this can be said to possess any cunning whatsoever is beyond me, but I didn't write the rules.

The lower length limit was 22 inches, but a big river catfish can weigh more than one hundred pounds, and at some point the question becomes not, "Is this fish a keeper?" but, "Will that fish throw Elmer back?" Add to this the likelihood there might be beaver, muskrats, snapping turtles, or cottonmouths in those same holes, and you begin to understand why few seasoned noodlers can count up to ten on their fingers.

The areas approved for the experimental study were along the Fabius River system and the Mississippi River in extreme northeast Missouri and the St. Francis River on the "inside" of the Bootheel, along the Arkansas border. If fish populations were not adversely affected, the legal waters were to have been extended after 2009. Effects on the human population were not tracked by the Missouri Department of Conservation, but they might have drawn the attention of the annual Darwin Awards, where individuals are commended for acting so foolishly and fatally that they remove themselves from the human gene pool.

Ultimately the Department of Conservation determined that catfish stocks were being adversely affected, so noodling is again illegal everywhere in Missouri.

I chose the town of La Grange as the logical hub for this controversial hobby, not only because of its location but also because it has a gambling casino in town. I want people to consider carefully whether they would prefer gambling by sticking coins into a slot machine and yanking on the handle or by sticking their hands in the jaws of a one hundred pound flathead and seeing if they can handle what happens.

The Town That Cement Built

When Hannibal residents mention this place, you might easily think they are telling you something about Alaska. But the name of the old town of Ilasco is an acronym for the ingredients used to make cement: iron, lime, alumina, silica, calcium, and oxygen. This company town of the Atlas Portland Cement Company was home to a host of immigrant groups, mostly from Eastern Europe, and from here they supplied most of the cement used to build the Panama Canal and the Empire State Building.

Ilasco can still be found on many maps, but the town proved less durable than the product its residents once manufactured. Atlas Portland dismantled the town years ago; now all that remains is a lonely plaque that stands along the highway in tribute to the immigrant families who lived and worked there.

As you leave Hannibal driving south on MO 79, pause for a moment at the Ilasco memorial about a mile out of town and give thanks to the anonymous men and women who did so much to build America.

A MISSOURI TABLE WINE

SWEET
LOUISIANA BASYE

ONE LEGEND REPORTS THE BIRTH OF
LOUISIANA BASYE ON THE DAY
OF THE LAND PURCHASE BY THE SAME NAME.
HER FAMILY LOCATED TO THIS AREA IN 1816.
THE SETTLERS WERE SO SMITTEN
WITH THE 13 YEAR OLD
THEY NAMED THE TOWN IN HER HONOR.

TROPICAL FRUIT BLEND AND A FLORAL AROMA, FINISHES SEMI-DRY.

EAGLE'S NEST

Louisiana Basye was so sweet she had an entire town (and a wine) named for her.
EAGLE'S NEST WINERY

✴ ✴

Be Good, and You Might Have a Whole City Named for You

Louisiana

The city of Louisiana is not named for the vast, historic purchase that Thomas Jefferson made from Napoleon. Well, not directly, anyway.

Walter Basye, the attorney said to have authored the actual document of the Louisiana Purchase (working under Robert R. Livingstone and James Monroe), supposedly named his daughter Louisiana because she was born on the day of the famous land purchase in 1803. In 1816 the Basyes moved to a newly formed settlement on the Mississippi River in territory that is now northeast Missouri. The story goes that when the town fathers got together to decide on a name for the town, they were so taken with the sweetness of Walter Basye's teenage daughter that they named the town for her.

As if that weren't enough to fill a girl's head, the local Eagle's Nest Winery now cranks out bottles of a pretty good sweet white wine, which they also have named for Walter Basye's charming child. So raise your glasses high and make a toast to Sweet Louisiana Basye! She must have been quite a gal.

Stark Raving Glad

Louisiana

Visit the Louisiana Area Historical Museum and they will show you an old, as yet unrestored, larger-than-life-size portrait of Queen Marie of Rumania holding a Stark's Golden Delicious apple. The painting was made from a photograph, which the Queen at first refused to allow. But when she saw how much members of her royal party enjoyed the new variety of apples given to her by Stark's, she summoned the photographer back. The Queen's photograph and the story of how she was won over were included for many years in the Stark's catalog as a testimonial to the aptly named Golden Delicious.

In 1816, long before Queen Marie was born, James H. Stark established the first commercial nursery in America. By 1966, when Stark

Brothers' Nursery celebrated its 150th anniversary, six generations of the Stark family had served the business and it was the largest nursery in the world. The Stark Brothers' nursery catalog was the first to be published in color. Clarence Stark also used to slip in portraits of Shakespeare and Shakespearean quotes.

Famed horticulturist and plant breeder Luther Burbank credited the Stark family with making his work profitable. In return he joined with Thomas Edison to support patent legislation for plant breeders. That law revolutionized agriculture and made the Stark family richer still. Toward the end of his life, Burbank directed his wife to place the dozens of unmarketed varieties he still held with Stark Brothers after his death.

You have no idea how much money Stark Brothers generated, unless you find a longtime resident to point out how many mansions in town were built by members of the Stark family. (They are not on any official tour.) No longer an agricultural empire but a more modest nursery in other private hands, Stark's is still a visible presence around Louisiana. The nursery still features exclusive varieties of fruits any gardener or gourmet will recognize.

The best way to trace the Stark Brothers and Luther Burbank legacies is at the Louisiana Area Historical Museum at 304 Georgia Street (573-754-5550), which contains a treasure trove of Luther Burbank's personal papers. The museum is in the process of expansion and reorganization. During this time it is open seasonally, or by appointment. Be sure to stop by if you are in town. Call the Louisiana Chamber of Commerce at (573) 754-5921 for more information.

A Larger-Than-Life Lady
Memphis

When Ella Ewing was born March 9, 1872, she appeared to be a normal, healthy child in every way. But unbeknownst to anyone, a tumor was growing on her pituitary gland. By the age of seven, Ella began to grow "faster than the corn," as her father used to say. Before

The Handsomest City's Darkest Crime

During the Civil War the Confederate sympathizers in Missouri lived mostly in the northern part of the state, while the Union sympathizers were concentrated in larger cities and southern Missouri. This was because Southerners had settled mostly where the best farmland was to be found.

By 1860 Palmyra had so many gracious Southern-style homes that it was often called "the Handsomest City in North Missouri." During the Civil War Palmyra was far from most of the action, but a small garrison of Union troops was stationed there to prevent problems from the numerous Confederate sympathizers. All was quiet until October 18, 1862, when ten local Confederate prisoners, guilty of mostly minor offenses, were summarily executed on the orders of Union colonel John McNeil, who was upset that a Confederate colonel had not returned a captured pro-Union civilian.

The executions were carried out in grisly fashion and badly botched. Both Jefferson Davis and Abraham Lincoln called the Palmyra Massacre "the Darkest Crime of the Civil War." The fairgrounds where the murders took place were never used again. Today a memorial marks the spot locals still call "the Old Fairgrounds" at the Palmyra city limits, just off Ross Street on the east side of town.

★ ★

she died at the age of forty, Ella reached a height of 8 feet, 4 inches and weighed 277 pounds. Although she was known far and wide as the Missouri Giantess, neighbors in the little town of Gorin where she grew up and folks in the rest of Scotland County referred to her respectfully as "Miss Ella."

At the age of twelve, Ella outgrew her 5-foot-6-inch mother. By the time she was fourteen, she was as tall as her 6-foot-2-inch father. In the year between she had a traumatic experience when she was chosen to read the Declaration of Independence for the Wyaconda Fourth of July celebration. People gawked so openly at the poor child that she broke down in tears; her father swore she would never again be made a public spectacle.

The manager of a Chicago museum convinced the family that nineteen-year-old Ella could make profitable appearances where she would be respectfully treated. Ella earned $1,000 for her thirty days in Chicago, and thereafter she made numerous appearances at fairs and shows closer to home. In 1897 Miss Ella was quoted in the *St. Louis Post-Dispatch,* saying that she had learned to love exhibition life.

Accounts vary, but it seems that Ella traveled rather extensively in the United States and Canada, appearing with both Buffalo Bill's Wild West Show and the P. T. Barnum Circus. At a typical appearance, the public paid 10 cents for a look, 10 cents to snap a photo, and the whopping price of 25 cents to shake the Missouri Giantess's hand. With the money she earned, Ella helped her parents move from their small cabin in the woods to a large home with high ceilings and 9-foot doorways.

Several marriage proposals were made, but the suitors' sincerity and motives were in doubt, so Miss Ella remained single. She died on January 10, 1913, as a result of her pituitary disorder. She had wished to be cremated to avoid having her body stolen and displayed, which was not an uncommon fate for famous people of that time. Her father could not bear the thought of cremation, however, so after a specially arranged funeral, she was buried in a cemetery just 4 miles from her home in Gorin. Her coffin was encased in cement to prevent theft. There the great lady's remains reside today.

The best place to recall the life of Ella Ewing is at the Downing House Museum in Memphis, Missouri. There is a life-size model of Ella, plus her 9-foot iron bed, a chair she used, a glove, and one of her shoes. Schoolchildren seem most fascinated with the glove and the shoe, but younger children will probably just run up and hug the big model's legs. Miss Ella would be happy her memory still inspires love.

Memphis is at the junction of MO 15 and US 136 in Scotland County. The Downing House Museum is located at 311 South Main Street and is open May through October only. Call (660) 465-2259 for details.

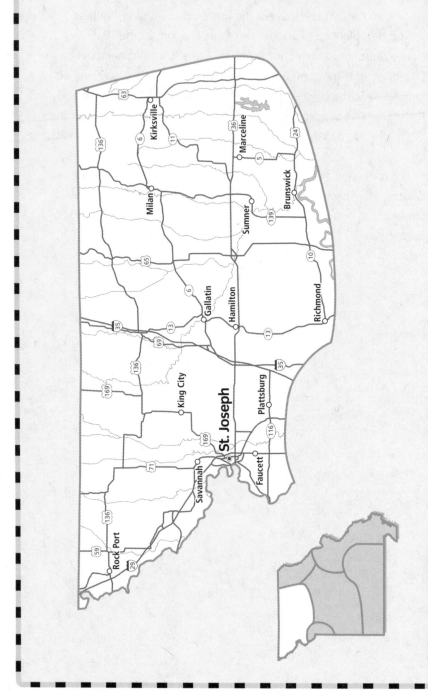

Northern Prairie

3

Northern Prairie

Glaciers came down and crushed the northern third of Missouri several times in the past 300 million years or so. When they finally pulled out for the last time, they left behind some terrific soil and the beautiful Missouri River. French and Amish and other German immigrants rushed into the Grand and Chariton Valleys, once they were opened for settlement by the Louisiana Purchase. Other prime farmland in the region was snapped up by wealthy Southerners, who had distinctly Confederate sympathies during the Civil War. Much of the region, particularly to the west, lives on the legacy of the Pony Express, which was headquartered in St. Joseph. That multimillion-dollar debacle, which didn't even last two years, was ironically such a mass-marketing miracle that people still fall in love with the romance of the failed enterprise today. There is something about plucky little riders dodging danger on fast horses to get the mail through that captures the American imagination.

Today, more than 150 years after the Pony Express riders rode, towns far to the east of the easternmost station on the route still brag that they were once on the railroad line that delivered mail to the Pony Express riders, or that their farms produced the horses that carried the mail. Travelers in a hurry might miss noticing, but the region is still horse country. The legacy of proud people who raised, trained, and showed some of the finest horses in America is still in evidence.

★ ★

Completely Nuts

Brunswick

Missouri's native pecans are usually rather small but very tasty. South-erners are driving up here all the time, saying that ours are good but theirs are bigger. In 1955 George James discovered a hardy, thin-shelled giant pecan, which he patented as the Starking Hardy Giant. To draw attention to his find, he put on display a giant reproduction, which he titled the World's Largest Pecan—12,000 pounds worth. Okay, so it is cement and wouldn't taste very good, but nobody, and

The World's Largest Pecan weighs about 12,000 pounds.
HARRY ROGERS CO.

I mean nobody, has got one bigger. This sucker is 7 feet in diameter and 12 feet long. Let's see someone try to top that!

See the World's Largest Pecan and visit the George James Pecan Museum at the Nut Hut, James Pecan Farms, 3 miles east of Brunswick on US 24. They sell all kinds of edible goodies and nutty souvenirs. Open year-round. Free.

Gimme a Sign

Faucett

The Farris Truck Stop in Faucett hadn't been open too long in 1976 when the owners decided they needed some signage. Not wishing to do things in a small way, they hooked a 1974 Peterbilt truck to a 1965 Fruehauf trailer and mounted the sucker on steel pillars set in 60 yards of steel-reinforced concrete. The whole trucking thing

When I said "Put her up on the lift," I didn't mean quite so high.
HARRY ROGERS CO.

rises some 50 feet in the air and has withstood more than a quarter
century of winds whipping off the prairie. If you stop after dark and
the motel has no vacancy, I suppose you might try to sneak over and
shinny up to spend the night in the truck's sleeper. But watch that
first step when you get up in the night.

The truck stop is on I-29, south of St. Joseph. You can't miss the
sign.

Squirrel Cage Jail

Gallatin

No, it isn't illegal to be a squirrel in Daviess County. The rotary, or
"squirrel cage," jails were an invention of the Pauley Jail Building and
Mfg. Company of St. Louis back in the latter half of the nineteenth
century. Only six of these innovative incarceration contraptions are
thought to have been built, and only three of those still stand.

Rotary jails were intended to provide better security by limiting
access to and from the eight cells inside. A round "squirrel cage"
revolved on a single axis inside a perimeter of stationary bars. Unfortunately, sanitation, winter heating, and the hand-crank mechanism
all presented significant problems, so the idea never really caught on.

The octagonal Daviess County rotary jail was built for a total cost
of $11,261.15 and completed in 1889. Women's cells were located
upstairs in the attached sheriff's residence. With a few modifications
to correct the problems mentioned above, the squirrel cage jail was
kept in service until 1975. (The original squirrel cage mechanism was
dismantled in 1964 for safety reasons.)

Although the James Gang was very active in Daviess County, Frank
James was acquitted in 1882 and was thus deprived of residing in the
squirrel cage. Today, while still undergoing renovations, the jail and
former sheriff's residence serve as a museum and are on the National
Register of Historic Places.

The jail is located on West Jackson Street in Gallatin. Open seasonally. Call (660) 663-2154 for more information.

"Nuts!" was one of the gentler expletives used by criminals locked up in the squirrel cage jail.

A Penney Saved

Hamilton

A psychologist once told me, "Almost anyone with the first or last name of Penny will be careful with a dime." That was certainly true of J. C. Penney, whose middle name, after all, was Cash. The American entrepreneur from Hamilton is credited with revolutionizing the American retail industry by stressing the Golden Rule. Such respect for his customers and his workforce, plus his attention to detail, allowed Penney to build a chain of department stores that prospered even through the Great Depression.

Penney refused to have any memorials in his name during his lifetime, but the J. C. Penney Boyhood Home and Museum outside Hamilton and the J. C. Penney Museum and Library in town do a good
job of keeping his memory alive in his hometown today. Among
other things you'll learn is how, as a youngster, he tried to keep a
few hogs to raise money until the neighbors complained about the
smell. But no one complained when, as a rich man, Penney built an
agricultural showplace famous for registered livestock just outside
town. The J. C. Penney Company Store in Hamilton, which opened in
1924 and closed in 1981, is still visible today, although it now houses
the local hardware store.

Penney's boyhood home is at 312 North Davis (open year-round;
816-583-2168). Then stop by the museum and library downtown.
Don't miss Penney's beautiful 1946 Cadillac convertible, which is
parked in its own special garage next to the Conoco Station at the
junction of US 36 and MO 13.

Superlative Rivers

Most Americans would guess that the
Mississippi River is the country's longest. Wrong. While the Mississippi is
North America's largest river, she is
only 2,340 miles long. Her major tributary, the Missouri, outdistances
her by 200 miles, stretching from Three Forks, Montana, for 2,540 cur-
vaceous miles to her confluence with the Mississippi at St. Louis. The
Missouri's circuitous path, plus their persistent belief that she would
ultimately lead them on the most direct path across the continent, was
one reason that Lewis and Clark took so long to complete their expedition (1803–1806).

High Prices of Gas
King City

The price of gasoline keeps going up, but you will probably never see a pump price higher than on the Big Pump in King City—it's two stories tall. The Tri-County Historical & Museum Society displays this roadside attraction at 508 North Grand Avenue, at the junction with US 169. The museum serves as a repository for the kind of weird and unrelated stuff that local people don't want anymore, but on the way to the dump or a yard sale, others will say, "You can't get rid of THAT!" A perfect example is the antique permanent wave machine, which graced somebody's beauty parlor during the Depression. It's a big drum, with lots of scary wires hanging off it, which used to get hooked up to ladies' hair. Think *Bride of Frankenstein.*

You'll find tools, old household appliances, and record books people didn't want to throw away. Even the Big Pump itself used to be over at Maryville. They decided to get rid of it, so it ended up at King City with the rest of the growing and, shall we say, eclectic collection. The museum is open Saturday and Sunday afternoons, plus holidays, from Memorial Day through September. During the rest of the year, you can just drive by and gawk at the World's Largest Gas Pump.

The Art of Imagination
Marceline

People in Marceline will tell you that if you take a map of their downtown and lay it over a map of "Main Street, U.S.A." in Disneyland, they match up exactly. This actually makes sense, as Walt Disney spent his boyhood in Marceline, a town he always loved. "I'm glad I'm a small town boy, and I'm glad Marceline was my town," he wrote to the *Marceline News* in 1938. At the time of his death, Disney was reportedly still toying with the idea of creating a "small town" theme park or attraction outside Marceline.

Not only the street pattern translated to Disneyland. Disney's legendary love of trains is said to have begun when he watched the trains pulling in and out of the station here, and his inspiration for the Matterhorn and its roller-coaster ride was said to come from a slag heap and coal cars at the town's coal mine, visible from his upstairs bedroom window. Now that's what I call a fertile imagination! At Disney's direction, the Midget Autopia, the first ride retired from Disneyland, was relocated to Marceline. (The vintage cars can no longer be driven, but one is on display.) Over the years Disney returned frequently to visit, and he made numerous contributions to the local elementary school and the town. Today the old depot serves as a museum dedicated to the memories of Walt Disney and his brother, Roy.

The slag heap is gone, but Disney's memory lives on in Marceline. There are several things to see and do around town, and the choices change frequently.

The Walt Disney Hometown Museum is open Tuesday through Sunday from May through October. Visit www.waltdisneymuseum.org or call (660) 376-3343 for details.

One Foot in the Grave

Milan

I guess you could say poor Pete Kibble got a step ahead of himself.

As a young man Pete lost a foot in a railroad accident. Such painful incidents were not uncommon back in the days of the railroads. Wounds healed. Life went on. Doctors had, fortunately or unfortunately, learned much about prostheses during the Civil War, so Pete was fitted with a serviceable replacement for his lost appendage.

But Pete, having lived in Milan all his life, expected to live out his life and die there. So, not wishing to be eternally separated from his foot, Pete had it buried in the Oakwood Cemetery high atop Milan's prettiest hill. A simple stone marker marks the spot with the tasteful inscription, PETE KIBBLE'S FOOT—1917.

★ ★

Then Pete's life took unexpected turns. He had the opportunity to travel west in search of a better fortune. He hopped around a bit, but he never got back to die in Milan as he intended. Pete died and was buried in Arizona, without his long-anticipated reunion ever taking place.

Today nobody knows exactly what happened to the rest of Pete. The old-timers I talked to couldn't agree whether it was Montana, Wyoming, Colorado, or Arizona where Pete met his Waterloo. Finally I located an elderly nephew who told me he was sure it was Arizona, but he couldn't be more specific than that.

Kibble's foot may have kicked the bucket, but luckily the rest of Kibble did not.

★ ★

Nobody in Milan knows if Pete died with family out there or if anybody visits his grave today. But the kids in Milan always stop by on Halloween to set the tone for their trick or treating. I'm sure they have stories about those footsteps they hear in the dark.

Milan is in the middle of Sullivan County on MO 6, west of Kirksville. When you drive into town, just keep going uphill until you reach the lovely Oakwood Cemetery. Pete's foot is southwest of the flagpole near the Haas family marker, just a few feet away (no pun intended).

Minute Rice
Plattsburg

At noon on March 4, 1849, the term of President James K. Polk expired. For deeply held religious beliefs, President-elect Zachary Taylor refused to be sworn in on the Sabbath, insisting instead that the ceremony be held at 11:30 Monday morning. The outgoing vice president, George M. Dallas, had resigned the previous Friday. So according to the Succession Law of 1792, David Rice Atchison, the presiding officer of the Senate, automatically became president of the United States to fill the void. Or some say.

Almost as much debate has waged over this point as it did over hanging chads following the presidential election of 2000. Some scholars claim that as Atchison's own Senate term expired on March 3 and he would not be sworn in for his next term until March 5, he was not officially a senator on March 4 and therefore could not reasonably be assumed to fill the vacancy. Others contend that barring removal or resignation, an elected official holds that office until a successor is duly sworn in. Atchison, who was immensely respected by his Senate colleagues, being elected president pro tem sixteen times (fourteen times unanimously), apparently did not care greatly about the question. By his own account some years later, he had been extremely tired following the flood of work to be done at the end of the session and so had retired and slept through most of his twenty-three-and-a-half-hour "term" as president of the United

★ ★

States. His detractors have implied that Atchison was fond of strong spirits and that he spent the time sleeping off a drunken binge.

The one-day president did ascend to another higher office subsequently in his career. On April 18, 1853, President Franklin Pierce's vice president, William R. King, died while in office, and Atchison filled that vacancy until December 4, 1854. About that fact there seems to be no debate.

A statue of Atchison stands at the entrance to the Clinton County courthouse in Plattsburg.

The Morel Majority

Richmond

The late Charles Kuralt once called a friend of mine who is a nationally recognized authority on foraging for wild foods.

"Mrs. Tatum, this is Charles Kuralt," the folksy CBS television journalist began, "I have seen you on *The Tonight Show,* and I have read your book. I'm in the area for a few days, and I would like to come out and interview you."

"I'm sorry," BJ scarcely let the man finish before telling him, "the morels are up."

"I beg your pardon," Kuralt chuckled, thinking he had not allowed the significance of his name to sink in before asking to meet. "I guess you didn't understand me. This is Charles Kuralt," he said slowly, with great emphasis.

"I know who you are," BJ cut him off. "You are that 'Off the Wall' person." (BJ doesn't watch a lot of television, so Off the Wall sounded as right as "On the Road.") "You didn't understand me, Mr. Kuralt," she said firmly and slowly, as though he were hard of hearing. "The morels are up. I don't have time for you."

Kuralt might have been baffled, but we morel aficionados have no trouble understanding her decision. When the morel mushrooms are up, and even for weeks beforehand, fungus fanatics can think of little else.

★ ★

Finding fabulous fungi to fry is only one reason to celebrate Richmond's Mushroom Festival.

People will talk for hours about the best kinds of places to hunt mushrooms and the sure signs they are ready to pop up (I watch for the emerging dogwood blossoms), but none of us will share where we actually find the elusive delicacy.

At the Richmond Mushroom Festival each year, you can gather with thousands of fellow fans of fungi to celebrate this rite of spring. Held the first weekend in May, it's not just a great place to buy T-shirts, posters, and bumper stickers. It's also a great gathering— even for people who won't eat mushrooms on their pizza.

The incredible range of activities includes carnival rides, live music, dancing, a fine arts show, a golf tournament, a fun run, a talent contest, selection of Little Mr. & Mrs. Mushroom, Humane Society animal adoptions, and a demolition derby. All this to celebrate a quiet pastime that causes people to take long, secretive walks in the deep woods, alone.

Come to think of it, with all that going on, the Richmond Mushroom Festival sounds like somebody's brilliant idea to keep everybody else out of the woods when the morels are at their peak.

Richmond is just over half an hour east of Kansas City, at the junction of MO 13 and MO 10. For more information visit http://richmondchamber.org or call (816) 776-6916.

Missouri's Windy City
Rock Port

Talk about turning lemons into lemonade. Prairie winds were said to cause lonely pioneer women to go insane. The winds can be relentless. But now that pleases the 1,300 citizens of Rock Port, because the winds that whip across the prairie and through their little town generate more than enough electricity to supply all the town's electrical needs. The extra power generated by four wind turbines within city limits goes back into the electrical grid to be used by other communities. That sounds pretty sweet to me.

This achievement in 2008 led Rock Port to be designated the country's first 100 percent wind-powered community. With maps showing Missouri's northwest corner containing the state's most abundant wind resources, Rock Port is serving as a good example to area farmers and other local communities to try and catch the wind.

There are federal subsidies involved, and the turbines are actually owned by John Deere's wind power division. When you get into the technical aspects of the project, there are fractions of pennies calculated per kWh (kilowatt-hour), lease agreements, and transmission lines to take into consideration.

Rock Port looks for a pot of gold under a rainbow with wind power.
ERIC CHAMBERLAIN

Had he thought much about all of that, Eric Chamberlain, who most folks give credit for turning them on to this bright idea, might have just let it float away on a breeze. Other community leaders soon got swept up in Eric's enthusiasm, however, and before they quite realized it, the turbines were whirling.

Many changes can be expected in the energy landscape during the twenty years those first four turbines are expected to last. To see a little town on the frontier of those changes, visit Rock Port in extreme northwest Missouri, at the juncture of I-29 and US 136. For more information e-mail eric@windcapitalgroup.com or call the Rock Port City Hall at (660) 744-2636.

A Big Champion

St. Joseph

In the world of midget wrestling, no one stands taller than Little Tokyo, aka Shigeru Akabane. I'm not saying that he is the biggest of the midget grapplers, mind you. But probably none in his class have had such a long, distinguished, and successful career. Born, raised, and turning pro in Japan about 1970, Little Tokyo married in Japan and was invited to St. Joseph by a wrestling promoter in 1972. His youngest son, Eddie, remembers that sometimes he would not see his dad for months at a time, except for watching him wrestle on television.

Little Tokyo retired to make cowboy hats at the Stetson factory.
SHIGERU AKABANE

★ ★

Little Tokyo became the world champion midget wrestler, holding the belt in the early 1980s, and he participated in the prestigious "Wrestlemania 3," which he still lists as one of his proudest achievements in the ring. He had a bit part in the 1970s kung fu movie *Black Samurai,* and he wrestled in a pro bout as recently as 2001. (I'm about the same age, but I've made a resolution not to wrestle with anything stronger than my laundry.)

Long stints on the road and a job some would characterize as "violent" obviously did not prevent Shigeru from developing close family ties. In a beautiful online tribute, Eddie Akabane called his father "a man of many talents and . . . special gifts" and went on to say, "He is not only my father but more importantly my friend."

In semiretirement the Japanese gentleman many know only as Little Tokyo worked at the Stetson factory, where he made cowboy hats and other headgear. His son says for relaxation his father drinks a little beer. If you see the champ at a family tavern in St. Joe, you'd better buy him a round. This is a guy you want on your side if a fight breaks out.

Death Takes a Tour
St. Joseph

The Heaton-Bowman-Smith and Sidenfaden Chapel funeral home is the oldest continually operated business in St. Joseph, as well as the oldest funeral home in Missouri. And they show no signs of going under.

Beginning as the Heaton Undertaking Ware Rooms in 1842, this funeral home moved around town, arriving at its current location in 1968. Here the owners realized they had in their attics what they called "a treasure of interesting artifacts from funeral service practiced many years ago." They created the museum to present a historical perspective on the funeral industry in general.

Among their most popular items are the basket used to transport the body of Jesse James to the undertaker and the ledger recording

★ ★

his funeral. There's an ice-cooled casket from the early nineteenth century, a time before embalming when bodies were actually put "on ice." Antique metal coffins are also here, with small windows through which mourners could view their dearly departed. Other displays describe—very respectfully—how human remains have been prepared for burial in America for more than 150 years.

The museum, at 3609 Frederick Avenue, is free and open year-round, but call (816) 232-3355 prior to your arrival. Tours last approximately forty-five minutes.

Complete Lunacy
St. Joseph

People complain about the way mentally ill patients are treated today, but it is nothing compared with the shocking treatment they once received. George Glore created the Psychiatric Museum in 1968 to educate the public on issues of mental health and how its treatment has progressed over the centuries.

The museum displays full-size replicas of devices used for therapy from the sixteenth century through modern times. Long (and not so long) ago, people with mental illnesses were confined in cages, dropped into icy water, and sometimes shut inside big spinning wooden wheels. Anthropological finds reveal that several ancient cultures believed that evil spirits might be released by cutting into a person's skull. More-modern treatment methods on display show that we are certainly making progress but still have a long way to go.

Some of the more encouraging and inspirational exhibits demonstrate the fine work and artistry performed by residents of the Northwest Missouri Psychiatric Rehabilitation Center, once known as State Lunatic Asylum No. 2. Teenagers in a residential program refurbished two junked cars into really cool hotrods that won auto show awards for design; these, too, are on display. You'll go in thinking the museum is going to be creepy, but you'll come away with a whole

All too capable-looking, these nurses worked in
State Lunatic Asylum No. 2 circa 1900.
GLORE PSYCHIATRIC MUSEUM

new respect for the patients and professionals in the field of mental health. I guarantee you will be crazy about this place.

The Glore Psychiatric Museum is located at 3406 Frederick Avenue, St. Joseph. Open Monday through Saturday 10:00 a.m. to 5:00 p.m. and Sunday 1:00 to 5:00 p.m. One small admission covers three museums at the site. Visit www.stjosephmuseum.org/glore.htm or call (800) 530-8866 for more information.

Not So Sweet Home
St. Joseph

Some people consider Jesse James an outlaw and a cold-blooded killer. Others defend him as a Robin Hood, changed for the worse by the Civil War. Stories and rumors surrounding the life and death of Jesse James have caused him to become one of the most famous

A bullet hole befitting a legend.

people in the world, more recognizable abroad than many of our nation's leaders and more upstanding citizens.

Whatever your opinion, you'll doubtless be shocked and horrified when you tour the Jesse James Home Museum and see for yourself the bullet hole in the wall made when fellow gang member Bob Ford shot and killed Jesse for the $10,000 reward. Everyone agrees that Ford couldn't have beaten Jesse in a fair fight, so he and his brother, Charlie, waited until Jesse was on a chair with his back turned, straightening and dusting a framed embroidery that his mother had made. He wanted it to look nice because she was coming to visit.

After Jesse's death the Ford brothers were denied their reward and charged with murder themselves. Only a pardon from the governor released them. Charlie Ford later committed suicide, and Bob was killed in a barroom brawl. Rumors that Jesse James had somehow survived the attack persisted until as late as 1995, when DNA tests proved with "99.7 percent certainty" that it was indeed Jesse James who was shot in his home on April 3, 1882.

The Jesse James Home Museum is now located a short distance from where it stood when the murder took place. Visit it at Twelfth and Penn. Small admission charged. Call (816) 232-8206 for information.

Jump Mail
St. Joseph

Guides at the Pony Express Museum like to call their stable "the best little horse house west of the Mississippi." The Pony Express was a great idea when the first brave riders jumped on their fast horses to gallop along dangerous trails with lightweight packets of mail. They did deliver mail faster than anybody could imagine it back then, but the service lasted just a little over a year and a half, and the investors went famously in debt. Trains and the telegraph made the Pony Express obsolete almost overnight, yet the romance of the legendary riders lives on.

PONY EXPRESS RIDER'S OATH

"I, _____, DO HEREBY SWEAR, BEFORE THE GREAT AND LIVING GOD, THAT DURING MY ENGAGEMENT, AND WHILE I AM AN EMPLOYEE OF RUSSELL, MAJORS AND WADDELL, I WILL, UNDER NO CIRCUMSTANCES, USE PROFANE LANGUAGE, THAT I WILL DRINK NO INTOXICATING LIQUORS, THAT I WILL NOT QUARREL OR FIGHT WITH ANY OTHER EMPLOYEE OF THE FIRM, AND THAT IN EVERY RESPECT I WILL CONDUCT MYSELF HONESTLY, BE FAITHFUL TO MY DUTIES, AND SO DIRECT ALL MY ACTS AS TO WIN THE CONFIDENCE OF MY EMPLOYERS. SO HELP ME GOD."

Historical accounts do not indicate that this oath significantly improved anyone's behavior.
PONY EXPRESS MUSEUM

You'll learn a lot about the how and why of this whole enterprise when you tour the Pony Express National Museum. Advance publicity was so good that the first rider was surrounded by crowds, who pulled out his horse's hair for souvenirs. That first trip, begun April 3, 1860, took successive relay riders thirteen days to convey the mail to Sacramento. The record time for any one transit was seven days and seventeen hours (somewhat augmented by the telegraph on the other end), when riders helped deliver Lincoln's 1861 Inaugural Address to the West Coast.

Riders, including the famous Buffalo Bill Cody, would jump on one of 400 $200 mounts (which was a lot of horseflesh back then) and ride all-out to the next station, where another rider would jump on a fresh horse with the mail pouch. For the first ten weeks, the Pony Express service ran once a week, moving to twice a week thereafter, with trips averaging ten days in summer and twelve to sixteen days in winter. But remember, that was before they had the Book of the Month Club and all this junk mail.

The Pony Express National Museum is open seven days a week year-round at 914 Penn Street, downtown St. Joe. For more information call (800) 530-5930 or visit www.ponyexpress.org.

Crazy about Animals
Savannah

Crazy is the word for it.

Yes, the name M'Shoogy's does mean crazy in Yiddish. But in any language, when two comfortably well-off people give up what some would call "everything" for a bunch of hapless, homeless animals, lots of folks would say they are certifiably nuts.

Gary and Lisa Silverglat started M'Shoogy's as a privately funded animal shelter at their home about twenty years ago. In the time since, it has grown to become perhaps the largest such facility in the country. As a "no kill" facility, the Silverglats estimate that to date M'Shoogy's has saved more than 15,000 animals from certain death.

Trivia

Spay and neuter your pets. Donate to a shelter if you can. M'Shoogy's would be a great place to start. Volunteer. Adopt an animal and give it love. Believe me, your love will be returned. Care. To do otherwise would be insane.

They give a twenty-four-hour commitment to their animal charges. They have poured vast sums of their own money into the project and have taken a total of only four days away from the sanctuary in these last two decades. Totally whacko.

At any given time they provide shelter to literally hundreds of dogs, cats, and even some wild animals. Attempts are made, with considerable success, to release their rehabilitated wild creatures back into environments where they can thrive. Many of M'Shoogy's charges live with health problems and disabilities for which the Silverglats and their volunteer staff members tenderly care. On average it costs about $50 per month to care for each animal, not counting medicine, and approximately $500 to "open the door" as the money-crunchers would say. Cuckoo.

These are by no means naive individuals. The Silverglats ran a very successful retail business in nearby St. Joseph. Their volunteers include people with plenty of family responsibilities and busy pro-fessional jobs. In their "spare" time, the folks at M'Shoogy's have helped pass permit laws and legislation against animal abuse and exploitation. I'm running out of words to say, well, *m'shoogy*.

But the money isn't endless. People's time is limited. And the need is great.

M'Shoogy's is open to the public for adoptions Saturday from noon to 4:00 p.m. and other times by appointment only. It is a lovely and heartwarming place to visit. As big as M'Shoogy's is, they operate almost always at full capacity (with more waiting), so please do not try to bring them another unwanted pet. Please do, however, tour and see some of their many dogs and cats available for adoption virtually at www.mshoogys.com and at 11519 State Route C in Savannah. Call (816) 561-1635 for more information.

World's Largest Goose
Sumner

You thought you were glad that cows can't fly, but that emotion is nothing compared with the feeling of relief you'll experience when you realize that Maxie, the 5,500-pound Canada goose, can't really take off and drop some whitewash in your eye.

Her 65-foot wingspan is perpetually on the downstroke, as though she is taking off in Sumner, the "Wild Goose Capital of the World." Maxie was put there to honor Swan Lake National Wildlife Refuge, a flyway sanctuary and stopover for huge numbers of migratory waterfowl.

Originally the refuge was planned with just ducks and that rare bird, the prairie chicken, in mind. This was during the dust bowl conditions of the 1930s, when Congress secured these 10,000-plus acres of wetland to ensure that migrating ducks could safely make their annual passage. When the refuge was opened in 1937, geese were still going elsewhere. But by 1941 a flock of about 800 geese landed at the refuge. They apparently told all their friends, because in one recent year an estimated 89,000 snow geese alone stopped over at Swan Lake. The refuge has many places to watch the birdies, including a cool observation deck made out of an old silo.

Ducks haven't stopped visiting just because their big cousins jumped in the water. The same bird count estimated the transitory mallard population at 75,000. No wonder the 118 eagles seen that

"Birdie, Birdie, in the sky; just be glad this one can't fly."
HARRY ROGERS COMPANY

year were bald; the stress level from all that honking and quacking must have been frightening, even to a bird of prey.

For more information call (660) 856-3323 or visit www.fws.gov/midwest/swanlake. To visit Maxie and Swan Lake Refuge by land, take MO 139 from Laclede, west of Chillicothe, 12 miles south to Sumner. If it is migration season, I recommend that you wear a wide-brim hat—and don't look up.

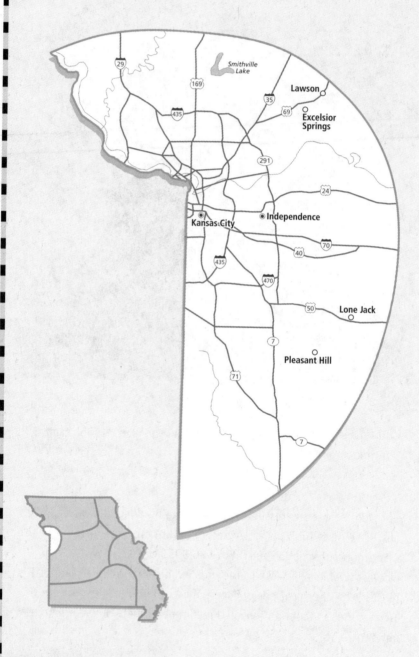

Around Kansas City

4

Around Kansas City

Cow Town. Some *Kansas City residents visibly flinch at the phrase, but others will proudly argue this is not only the original cow town but the standard to which all others should be measured. Kansas City—for years now the largest city in Missouri—isn't a small town by any means, but it is small-town friendly and cow-town cool.*

Originally just another fur-trading post established by the French, Kansas City soon came to dominate commerce on the upper Missouri River and the Santa Fe Trail. Supplies were purchased here for the long journeys westward, and everything from gold to farm commodities were sent back east through the Kansas City hub. When Union Depot was constructed in 1878, it was the second largest railroad depot in the world, and a lot of money was spent to make it the most splendid. Rail and river commerce still flow through Kansas City, but increasingly it is other industries, plus the draw of rich cultures, that drive this region's growth.

Inevitably Kansas City finds itself compared to St. Louis. When Kansas City finally surpassed St. Louis in size, the shouts could be heard all across the state. Despite its urban sophistication, cowboys still look comfortable and seem to fit into the mix in Kansas City. Cowboys in St. Louis just look weird.

★ ★

Taking the Waters
Excelsior Springs

Cities and towns that spend huge sums of money to remove trace minerals and bad-tasting chemicals from their water should take a lesson from Excelsior Springs. In the 1850s A. W. Wyman owned most of the land there, known as Olde Towne today, and one of his springs flowing into the Fishing River was so reddish and bad tasting that people called it "pizen." They claimed that if you drank the water it would kill you—or maybe cure you.

Local lore holds that a man named Travis Mellon brought his daughter there when nothing else had worked to cure her acute skin disease. Influenced by Indian beliefs that the spring had healing properties, Mellon had his daughter drink and bathe in the terrible-tasting water. When she was completely cured after only a few days of treatments, word spread rapidly. Soon people were using the spring to treat rheumatism, liver complaints, kidney disease, bladder disorders, dyspepsia, piles, and sciatica.

Wyman collaborated with his friend, the Reverend J. V. B. Flack of Missouri City, and they had the water tested in St. Louis. The report stated that the spring contained the highest concentration of iron ever discovered and that it might have medicinal properties. (This is from the same Nietzschean school of medical thought that teaches, "That which does not kill us makes us stronger.") Wyman and Flack named the spring Siloam and wasted no time in platting the town. By the 1880s the two men were selling lots—cheap, to encourage settlement. Within a year a hundred houses were built and another 1,000 people were living in tents nearby. A barrel sunk in the mud collected water from Siloam Spring, and a steady stream of visitors came to drink thereof. Mud baths became popular. Popcorn was sold at the spring to make people thirsty so that they would drink more water.

When Siloam Spring couldn't produce enough water for the demand, another spring, also producing iron manganese water, was found. Wells were drilled, eventually bringing the number of water sources to forty-six. Ultimately five different mineral waters were discovered, at different depths. The array of springs giving iron manganese, sulpho-saline, soda bicarbonate, calcium, and lithium waters was said to be the most varied in the world. Two wells in Excelsior Springs produced water so high in salt content that they could only be used for bathing and making bath crystals.

Following the spa fashions of the day, simple structures gave way to more elaborate Victorian ones. In 1917 architect Henry F. Hoit designed fabulous marble pavilions, beautifully landscaped by George E. Kessler. His designs also gave the evolving city a boulevard system and community parks totaling more than 2,000 acres, many still in existence. Between 1912 and 1933 the Interurban electric train line carried passengers between the springs and the Kansas City area at speeds exceeding 100 miles per hour.

At the height of the Great Depression, the city's leaders sought to revive their failing economy by applying to the federal government for a quarter of a million dollars to bring all the waters together in one building. In a classic example of federal largesse, they were told that the Works Progress Administration (WPA) did not make loans that small—and the grant was increased to $1,000,000. For that grand sum the city built the magnificent Art Deco Hall of Waters, containing the world's longest water bar.

Today you can visit these curious monuments to America's romantic era of healing waters. At the Excelsior Springs Historical Museum, you can separate fact from fiction and view the various ways the waters were once "taken." Several of the practices, such as baths and the drinking of certain mineral-rich waters, are being restored in a revival of the city's tourism industry.

To reach Excelsior Springs take US 69 northeast of Kansas City and continue east on MO 10. For more information call the museum at (816) 630-0101. Open Tuesday through Saturday 10:00 a.m. to 4:00 p.m. No admission charged.

Things Always Look Better After a Good Night's Rest

There's a famous photograph of Harry S Truman, taken after the presidential election of 1948, holding a newspaper. It was taken in front of the Elms Hotel in Excelsior Springs, where Truman had gone to await the results. Thomas E. Dewey was assumed by so many to be a shoo-in that several newspapers went to press early the night before with headlines declaring Dewey victorious. Truman had the last laugh.

No Hair-Brained Scheme

Independence

How many times have you heard a woman say, "I wish I could do something with this hair!"? Leila Cohoon, a take-charge gal, doesn't have that problem. With Leila there's never a hair out of place.

As a lifelong cosmetologist, Leila's mission was to beautify hair. Then she developed a fascination for hair art and began collecting. Eventually she decided it was her mission to display her treasures of tresses for all to see. Leila's Hair Museum grew and grew, and it keeps on growing.

The Victorians get credit for being the most meticulous in their methods of preserving hair. Today we might just save a lock of hair from Junior's first haircut and stick it in his baby book. But back in the nineteenth century, people wove elaborate hair wreaths containing contributions from every member of the family. Hair jewelry was also once quite the rage, although many of the methods for making such creations have been lost.

Leila is preserving both the artworks themselves and some of the even rarer sets of instructions and manuals on how they were made. Where no clear patterns existed, Leila sometimes took her lovely pieces of hair art apart to make note of the method of construction before carefully weaving them back together. Now she is an authority on how hair weaving was done. One of the masterpieces in the museum's collection is a floral tapestry dating back to 1853 that contains hair from 156 members of one family. Phyllis Diller, famous in a different way for amazing people with hair, heard of Leila's Hair Museum and contributed a hair wreath she owned.

Located at the Independence College of Cosmetology she founded, Leila's collection culled from coifs houses more than 200 hair wreaths and more than 2,000 pieces of hair jewelry. Leila thinks her museum "is possibly the only hair museum in the United States, maybe the world."

At Leila's Hair Museum (1333 South Nolan Road, Independence) walk-ins are always welcome. Open Tuesday through Saturday 9:00 a.m. to 4:30 p.m. Admission charged. Call (816) 833-2955 or visit www.hairwork.com/leila for information.

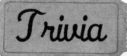

Trivia

Don't waste ink when you write the name of President Harry S Truman. His middle initial is just that—no period required. The "S" doesn't stand for anything, although some might think it stands for the expletive he was famous for using.

How Much Ground Can a Groundhog Cover?

Kansas City

One harbinger of springtime each year is the long-awaited appearance of Punxsutawney Phil, the Pennsylvania woodchuck whose ability to see—or not see—his shadow on February 2 seems to determine whether we will have an early spring or six more weeks of slush and snow. But runners raring to race need not worry what Phil's prediction portends. Even in subzero temperatures, after howling blizzards have dumped many feet of snow over the landscape, the annual Groundhog Run takes place in Kansas City. You don't even have to bundle up—the Groundhog Run takes place entirely underground.

Held early each year on the Sunday closest to Groundhog Day, this charity event takes place in the Hunt Midwest SubTropolis, the largest underground industrial park in the world. From a modest start in 1982, when a respectable $8,000 was raised for the Children's Therapeutic Learning Center, the Groundhog Run has speedily grown to bring in $250,000 in a single year and a total of $2.5 million over twenty-one years.

Aside from the worthy cause, runners love the novelty of running along wide, smooth road surfaces in perfect climatic conditions. A single loop of the underground course comprises the first 5-kilometer heat; runners wishing to compete in the subsequent 10-kilometer run simply complete two circuits.

Owned by Lamar Hunt, known to sports fans for his ownership of the NFL Kansas City Chiefs and the Wizards Soccer teams, the SubTropolis is 400 acres of underground buildings and roads carved out of 270-million-year-old limestone. The fifty or so local, national, and international companies located there cite low rent, utilities, and insurance costs combined with a high-security environment as reasons for their satisfaction. Runners are just happy to avoid the seasonal hazards of cold, wet, icy slop.

You don't have to be a runner to get to see the SubTropolis for yourself. Monday through Friday the complex is open for the public

The official mascot is always on hand to wish the athletes good luck.
CHILDREN'S THERAPEUTIC LEARNING CENTER

to drive through, free of charge, between 8:30 a.m. and 5:00 p.m. These are not guided tours, but the experience is a lot of fun in any weather. You will feel as though you are in a spy movie or a futuristic world.

The SubTropolis is located at 8300 Northeast Underground Drive, 1.5 miles east of the junction of I-435 and MO 210. For more information on the Groundhog Run, log on to www.childrenstlc.org or call (816) 756-0780 at least a month in advance; registration is limited.

★ ★

Cards by Joyce

Joyce Hall's parents named their son for the Reverend Joyce, the Methodist Episcopal bishop who visited their Nebraska town on August 29, 1891, the day Joyce was born. Unlike Johnny Cash's "Boy Named Sue," Joyce stayed out of fights, saying that a person learned to do that if he was smart enough. Instead, by the age of nine Joyce was selling perfume door to door. He soon switched to selling picture postcards. While still in his late teens, Joyce took a friend's advice and moved to Kansas City, where he lived at the YMCA and sold more picture postcards, which he kept in a shoebox under his bed.

A fire wiped out Joyce's expanding business in 1915, but he rebuilt; and by the time he died, the Hallmark company had 10,000 employees and annual sales of $300 million.

Not bad for a little shoebox business, Joyce.

Keep Your Eyes on the Birdies
Kansas City

They look for all the world as though some giant's children have been playing badminton out on the vast, well-groomed lawn and then carelessly left their shuttlecocks lying about when Nanny called them in for tea. The world's largest shuttlecocks are actually four sculptures by internationally famous artists Claes Oldenburg and Coosje van Brugen, commissioned by the Sosland family to be the first outdoor sculptures for the Nelson-Atkins Museum of Art.

The Nelson is a palatial building surrounded by elegant grounds, but somehow the supersize shuttlecocks seem right, although a bit zany, for that setting. Isn't it nice to know those smartsy-artsy people have a sense of humor?

You may romp around the Nelson-Atkins Museum of Art at 4525 Oak Street, off Forty-seventh Street just east of the Plaza. The museum is closed on Monday and Tuesday. Call (816) 751-1278 or visit www.nelson-atkins.org. Free admission to the permanent collection.

One of the four giant shuttlecocks left lying around the grounds of the Nelson-Atkins Museum of Art.

★ ★

Save a Connie
Kansas City

People who can identify every plane in flight the way ornithologists can spot birds on the wing will tell you that the Lockheed Super G Constellation was perhaps "the most beautiful aircraft to have graced the skies." In old movies—when a flight somewhere meant excitement, romance, or the sophistication of worldwide travel—directors would more often than not cut to a scene of a Constellation revving up, taking off, or sailing above cotton-candy clouds.

These old propeller-driven airplanes had not been manufactured since 1959, and by the 1970s most of those still in use had been grounded. In 1986 a group of air-flight enthusiasts who couldn't bear the thought of the Connie, as the plane was lovingly called, going extinct like the passenger pigeon banded together and founded the Save a Connie Foundation, making it their mission to find, acquire, make flyable, and restore a Lockheed Super G Constellation aircraft.

Finally a worthy specimen was located at Falcon Field in Mesa, Arizona, where the dry conditions worked in her favor. This cargo Constellation had been one of the last such planes to come off the Lockheed assembly line in 1959, serving first to haul cargo for Slick Airways and finishing her career as a bug sprayer in Canada before being retired to the Arizona desert in the mid-1970s.

Fortunately, too, there were still enough not-so-nice Connies and parts of Connies lying here and there to supply spare parts for the vintage plane. After nine weeks of rehab, the Connie took to the air again and flew to what would become her proud new home in Kansas City.

An assembled group of mostly retired TWA employees—including pilots, flight engineers, mechanics, and hostesses—went to work to refit the Connie as a passenger plane and to restore her to mint condition, complete with crew uniforms and galley items. TWA chipped in a brand-new paint job, and the *Star of America* was born.

The FBI Didn't Always Carry Heat

Today people flock to the marvelously restored Union Station in Kansas City to enjoy good restaurants, a variety of theaters, upscale shops, and the fascinating interactive displays of Science City. It's a great use of what was once the second largest train depot in the world.

But families out for fun rarely remember that this was also the scene of one of America's most daring and bloody gangland hits. Through the safety lens of time long passed, it is chilling and thrilling to think back on that fateful day, June 17, 1933. Frank Nash of the infamous Barker Gang was being escorted for transfer to Leavenworth Prison by two Kansas City police detectives, an Oklahoma police chief, and FBI Agent R. J. Caffrey. Their route through busy Union Station was supposed to be a closely guarded secret, but the word was out in the underworld that Nash should never reach his destination, for fear of his future testimony.

All four officers and their prisoner were ambushed in a hail of gunfire by three mobsters, including Charles Arthur "Pretty Boy" Floyd. Prior to that time FBI agents were not allowed to carry firearms, nor did they have the power to arrest. As a direct result of the "Kansas City Massacre," President Franklin Roosevelt immediately sought and received legislation to arm the FBI.

You'll feel completely safe in Union Station (30 West Pershing Road) today, but it is kind of exciting to remember this dangerous bit of the depot's colorful past. For more on Science City, visit www.sciencecity .com.

Today she is the main draw at the Airline History Museum, which also features a Martin 404 and a Douglas DC-3. But it is perhaps her appearances at air shows around the country that make the biggest impression. People witnessing a Connie takeoff are warned that "the large cloud of smoke and flames created when we start the engines is normal. No need to call the fire department." (This has apparently happened more than once.)

You can see the *Star of America* Connie and a whole host of flight hostess artifacts, airplane instruments, photos, and more at the Airline History Museum at the Kansas City Airport, 201 Northwest Lou Holland Drive, off US 169 north of Kansas City. Open seven days; admission charged. Call (800) 513-9484. A schedule of *Star of America* appearances at air shows is posted at www.ahmhangar.com.

Treasure in a Farm Field
Kansas City

If you were searching for gold, would you go digging in a Missouri cornfield? A couple of adventurous families who did just that found treasures beyond their greatest expectations.

The *Arabia* was only three years old that disastrous day in 1856 when an unseen walnut snag punctured her hull. She had been bound for Sioux City, Iowa, on a route that sometimes took her as far upstream as South Dakota. But snags in the river were the greatest threat to steamboats, responsible for an estimated 300 of the 400 recorded sinkings. Fortunately the *Arabia* lay grounded for several hours with enough of her decks above water that all the passengers and crew could get ashore using the only lifeboat on board. But before any of the more than 200 tons of cargo could be removed, the Missouri River took possession of the 171-foot paddle wheeler and carried her down.

Time passed, and the river gradually changed course. Swampy willow thickets became dryer ground and eventually cultivated farm fields. Thus it was that 132 years later, in a cornfield half a mile from

If it wasn't in the cargo aboard the steamship
Arabia, you probably didn't need it.
MISSOURI DIVISION OF TOURISM

★ ★

the current channel, the Hawley and Mackey families—organized as River Salvage, Inc.—found the *Arabia* 45 feet underground.

It took about two years to find and excavate the site in the late 1980s. The cornfield adventurers had been obsessed with gold, and they did find some, but they found even greater treasures in the everyday articles on board. Boxes, crates, and barrels packed with merchandise intended for retail trade on the frontier now serve as time capsules of that era on display at the Arabia Steamboat Museum. French perfume found on board still retains its delicate fragrance and is sold as souvenirs. One of many unexpected treasures is the hoard of antique buttons, still in mint condition. Be sure to ask how well whiskey and cognac survive after more than a century underground. The entire cargo may take twenty-five years to fully restore, so new exhibits are continually being added.

The museum is located at 400 Grand Boulevard in Kansas City. Tours take about ninety minutes. Admission charged. Call (816) 471-1856 or visit www.1856.com.

Not Hardly Gnarly Harley
Kansas City

Harley-Davidson motorcycles used to make you think of bad boys: James Dean, *Rebel Without a Cause,* Hell's Angels.

Well think again. Moms and grandmas ride Harleys. Retired couples take them on sightseeing trips. CEOs (of both sexes) ride their hogs home after work to unwind.

Tool on into the Harley-Davidson final assembly plant in Kansas City and you might not know whether you are at a motorcycle plant or a community-betterment association meeting. Most of the people I saw waiting to take the tour were middle age and middle class. There also were a few college kids and some young blue-collar types. Only one guy seemed to fit the old stereotype of a tough Harley biker, and when the lady tour leader started talking, I saw him help an older woman get up front where she could hear a little better.

Security was tight the day I was there. They were getting ready

Don't spit into the wind, and don't touch the employees'
motorcycles parked in front of the Harley-Davidson factory.

for a new model change, so some of the areas in the plant were off-limits. On a guided tour you'll spend about ninety minutes walking through the plant to see and hear how the XL product line is assembled. Afterward you can buy all kinds of Harley-Davidson gear and memorabilia—maybe get your mom a little cap made with denim, leather, and chrome.

The plant is located at 11401 North Congress, off I-29 just south of Kansas City International Airport. Call ahead (414-343-7850) for tour reservations (you must be twelve or older), offered Monday through Friday 8:00 a.m. to 1:00 p.m. Gift shop open (no appointment necessary) Monday through Friday 8:00 a.m. to 3:00 p.m.

Before Spandex
Lawson

Almost from the time in 1793 when Samuel Slater memorized the intricate designs of a British textile mill and illegally smuggled the revolutionary technology to America in his head, the United States was a dominant player in the worldwide textile industry.

New England streams first powered hundreds of mills. Later, cheap labor in the South caused many textile factories to move there. But through that time of transition, the demand for fabric in the Midwest and West allowed many profitable little mills to spring up closer to those markets. Even without access to abundant waterpower or cheap labor, the savings in transportation costs made midwestern textile mills competitive.

One such enterprise was the Watkins Mill, established by Waltus Watkins in the 1860s and viable for almost one hundred years. Like most small midwestern mills, the complex Watkins built also included an elegant home, fruit-drying shed, smokehouse, brick kiln, sawmill, gristmill, gardens, and orchards.

In 1964, following years of decline, the mill complex was acquired by the State of Missouri to operate as a state park. Today it is America's only 1860s woolen mill with all the original machinery still intact.

Filling a sizable three-story building, the early industrial machines were all powered by a sixty-horsepower slide-valve steam engine that Watkins purchased from a salvaged river steamboat.

Today the Watkins Mill complex is a fascinating time capsule of the Industrial Revolution in the Midwest. Maintained by a small staff and enthusiastic volunteers, the historic site is operated as a Living History Farm Program by men and women in period costumes, demonstrating how the entire mill complex worked.

A small lake, with many state park amenities, can complete a visit to historic Watkins Mill with a sudden plunge into twenty-first-century fun. There are few places where these two worlds are so pleasantly combined.

Watkins Mill State Park is off US 69, a short drive northeast of Kansas City. From Lawson follow signs to Park Road North. Open year-round. Call (816) 580-3387 or visit www.mostateparks.com/wwmill.

A Midwest Museum of the Middle East

Lone Jack

Americans seeking to learn more about Saudi Arabia and Bedouin culture should put Lone Jack at the top of their list. When Paul Nance and his wife, Colleen, returned to the United States in 1983 after working thirty-two years with an American oil company in Saudi Arabia, they brought with them a profound respect for Bedouin culture and a strong desire to inform the American public about this enigmatic people.

They created the Nance Museum to offer a window into a world unknown to most Americans. There you can see a virtually complete Bedouin tent home, used for forty years in the northern Saudi desert, and learn how resourceful Bedouins have been at recycling. There is a water bag made from a gazelle, with the legs serving as handles. The coffee cup holder is a World War I French artillery shell casing. Baskets are made from palm fronds. Scraps of wood are turned into

★ ★

**Paul Nance displays a portion of his amazing
collection of Bedouin objects.**
PAUL NANCE

bowls for camel milk. Coins become jewelry.

These curious artifacts, and many more, are presented by the
Nances in a context that educates Americans to the subtleties of
Saudi Muslim culture and its impact on our lives. This is not as
remote as some might think. When you graduated, you probably
proudly wore a gown, which is actually a form of the *bisht*, or cloak,
that came to us through Spain in respect for the great wisdom of
Muslims.

Bedouin culture was rich but largely unchanged until oil was discovered in Saudi Arabia. Much of the kingdom is still unchanged with regard to dress, religion, language, food preferences, and attitudes toward women. But with the largest known oil reserves in the world located there—and with 1.2 billion Muslim pilgrims wanting to visit Islam's holiest shrines at least once in their life—the country is under great pressures.

The Nance Museum in Lone Jack (US 50, east of Kansas City) is currently open by appointment only. Fee charged. Call (816) 697-2526.

Not So Pleasant
Pleasant Hill

The mural is beautiful in a dark, disturbing way. Perhaps only by confronting such poignant images can we truly appreciate the strong emotions and lasting legacy wrought by Civil War strife in Missouri. Divided within its own borders, almost a microcosm of the entire nation at that time, Missouri still occasionally reveals her scars left by the War Between the States.

Back Home: April 1865 by artist Tom Lea is one of several post office murals commissioned on various themes throughout the state of Missouri. Most of the others are cheerful, or at least focused on less-troubling themes. This scene, rendered in ash gray and black tones, shows the effects of Order #11, by which people living inside Cass County, Missouri, but more than 1 mile outside any of its three main cities were forced by Union troops to evacuate their homes during the Civil War. The vacated buildings were burned, and Union forces seized the remaining property.

In the picture the artist depicts three generations of a farm family, standing on a low rise beneath dark clouds. All that remains of their house is the chimney. Their farm fields lie in ruin. Their expressions are numb, and the mood is utterly quiet.

Missouri seems remarkable in its willingness to continue to lay bare such painful moments of a difficult history. Not all her public art is rendered in bright colors meant to please. Patriotism for the modern-day United States—as strong here as anywhere else in the country—is perhaps all the more remarkable when one sees the wasteland from which it grew.

Pleasant Hill is located at the junction of MO 58 and MO 7, east of Belton and south of Kansas City.

How Do You Wind This Thing?

Smithville Lake

Around 1976–77, when the Army Corps of Engineers was constructing the dam and dredging for Smithville Lake, they uncovered what is believed to be the remains of a wooden astronomical observatory. (A similar structure was unearthed and reconstructed near Cahokia Mounds across the Mississippi River from St. Louis in Illinois.) Work at the site was halted long enough for archaeologists to take measurements and samples. Now that the lake has been completed, a replica of this "Woodhenge" has been reassembled on its shores. Scientists from around the country have come to study the structure, particularly during the solstices and equinoxes.

Also at Smithville Lake, near the dam, rests a huge Sioux quartzite stone, deposited by the last glacier that stopped by, about 15,000 years ago. The uniqueness of this glacial erratic, as such stones are called, has led to speculation that the stone, in proximity to the observatory, might have had special significance to Paleolithic Native Americans and those who came later.

Nowadays, troglodyte American teens perform their own curious rituals upon the stone—usually after dark—layering it with inscrutable and sometimes all too discernible markings to record their deepest thoughts and highest aspirations.

To make your own observations, follow the signs, going north of MO 92 between Smithville and Kearney.

Ain't That Peculiar (If You've Ever Dealt with the Post Office)

The strangely named town of Peculiar, south of Kansas City in Cass County, got named in an odd way. In the late 1800s Postmaster E. T. Thomson was trying to set up the post office for his little community. He dutifully sent in an application and petition to the U.S. Post Office Department, requesting the name "Excelsior."

The department responded that the name was already taken by another community in Missouri and that Mr. Thomson should reapply with a new name. He did. That name was taken. He applied again. Name taken.

Finally, in frustration Mr. Thomson wrote that if the previous names were taken, would the Post Office Department kindly give his community some peculiar name—and he made the mistake of enclosing the word *peculiar* in quotation marks.

He received his commission from Washington—as postmaster of Peculiar, Cass County, Missouri.

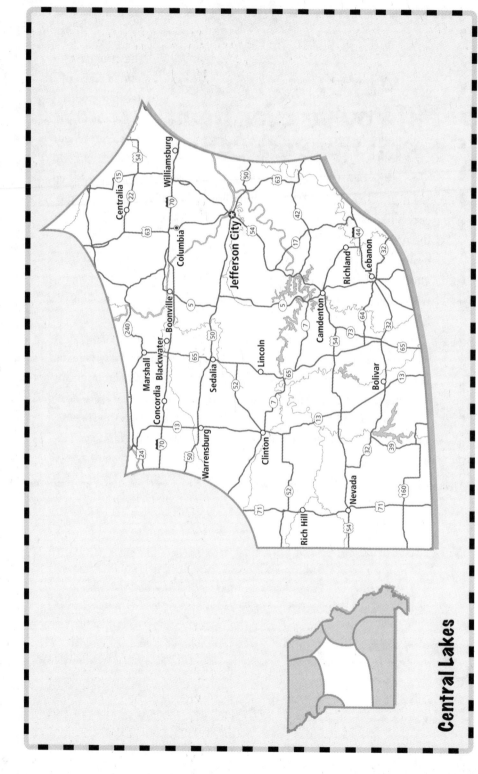

Central Lakes

5

Central Lakes

Rivers, dams, and *impoundments make central Missouri a playground for water-sports nuts from all over the Midwest. In every season, tourism here is dominated by happy people headed to, across, or back from "the river" or "the lake." Driving around the Central Lakes region, you are apt to see bumper stickers with sayings like "I'd Rather Be Fishing," "Water-skiers Do It Standing Up," and "My Other Car Is a Houseboat." Personal watercraft are considered truck accessories here.*

Lake of the Ozarks has been called "the Magic Dragon" because of the way its enormous, curved, and convoluted shape looks on the map. But this is also a farming region, and the Army Corps of Engineers is not universally beloved for the projects that were introduced to provide electrical power, water recreation, and flood control. Many family farms were submerged in the name of progress, and some communities that were promised a tourist bonanza found that their portions of the lakes were mere mudflats for most of the year.

Hunting is big here, too, and all kinds of trophy game have been recorded. Not long ago a hunter shot a thirty-six-point buck near Sweet Springs, drawing handsome offers from representatives of Bass Pro Shop's Outdoor World in Springfield, which would like to add the record rack to their impressive collection of animal trophies. Now questions have arisen as to who actually owns the dead deer, with rights to sell; the courts will have to decide.

A Charming Backwater

Blackwater

The tiny town of Blackwater was established in 1887, one of many towns along the Missouri Pacific Railroad Company's "river route" connecting Kansas City to Boonville, Jefferson City, and points east. The town was a water and coal stop for the steam-engine trains; the trains provided an export route for farmers' crops, dairy products, livestock, and a local rock quarry.

Things went along pretty swimmingly in Blackwater up through the years of the Great Depression, by which time the population had grown to about 650 people. Then diesel trains, which did not have to stop for water or coal, replaced the steam engines. Trucks and automobiles gave people other ways to transport goods and get places themselves.

About 1950 the Blackwater Stone Company hit springs when blasting for rock. The quarry flooded and the business closed. Blackwater had lost its largest employer, and the town slipped into a steep decline. At one point, residents feared most of the historic village might actually become a huge salvage yard. Today the hurried traveler along the interstate might think there is no reason to stop there.

But Blackwater has given birth to citizens with pride, imagination and fortitude. One family whose members had moved out of state bought several of the historic buildings downtown to save them from destruction. The Blackwater Preservation Society formed to create a vision, obtain grants, and seek tax credits for redevelopment.

The town elected Missouri's then youngest mayor, Bobby Danner, soon dubbed "the Barefoot Mayor" because he was so often found unshod when mainstream media folks came to interview him. Author and playwright Jay Turley, who was born in Blackwater, moved back to town and helped establish the West End Theatre in the old Baptist church. Proximity to I-70 and the historic towns of Arrowrock and Boonville brought bus tours and other interested outsiders to performances in town.

The Iron Horse Hotel in Blackwater treats guests to nineteenth-century luxury.

Today the renovated Iron Horse Hotel features gourmet dining and ten old-fashioned rooms reminiscent of the days when railroad travelers stopped for the night. In addition to their play performances, the West End Theatre sponsors wildly popular Haunted Hayrides on weekends in October and ragtime piano performances during December.

Although the population today is less than a third of what it was at its height, the citizens of little Blackwater can regale you with stories of their Mardi Gras celebrations and other impromptu events.

★ ★

Snickering

You might get a laugh over Blackwater's Snickers story. Sometime in the 1930s the Mars Candy Company held a contest to name a new candy bar (which they often did back then). Local folks say that Minnie Morgan, the druggist's wife, entered the contest with the name "Snickers" and won. Her prize was a tiny Austin automobile, so small it only had two seats. The car had such a narrow wheelbase that when Minnie would go careening too fast around a corner, the vehicle would flop over onto its side. Minnie would jump out, cussing and kicking the daylights out of the thing until two or three men would come and set it back upright for her. Then Minnie would go off, more or less merrily on her way.

There are countless clever murals around town, most painted by life-long resident and local historian Bonnie Rapp. When you visit, stay long enough to browse in the town's several antiques shops. Blackwater used to be home to one of the state's largest antiques wholesalers, and bargains still abound. I have never seen a town so small with as many public gardens and beautification projects. If you take time to look, you'll love what you see.

A good way to get oriented to Blackwater is to stop into the Bucksnort Trading Company on Main Street. Advertised as a "Step Back in Time," owners Gerald and Connie Cunningham have lovingly collected an eclectic array of period clothing, reenactors' supplies, Native American arts and crafts, music, instruments, herbs, books, and more, in keeping with Blackwater's rich past. If it is chilly, you may be invited to sit by the woodstove; if it's hot, you might be tempted to run barefoot around town.

Blackwater is not far off I-70; take exit 89 west of Columbia and Boonville. Visit www.blackwater-mo.com for more information and a virtual tour.

A Solution to Graffiti
Bolivar

Bolivar has done a clever thing that relates to art. Instead of getting all bent out of shape when kids go wild with paint, the city gave the kids a whole bridge to decorate. As you come driving into Bolivar on MO 32 off MO 13, you'll drive right under an old railroad overpass painted with a beautiful mural welcoming everyone to town. Part of the Rails to Trails recreation project, it's the result of local students unleashing their creativity instead of anger.

If anybody were ever to tamper with the mural, the kid grapevine is poised to identify the culprit, and it's expected that kids who have invested time and energy this way are more likely to be respectful of other people's property. The town is taking considerable pride in the work of its young citizens, and photographs of the painted bridge have already turned up on a few Web sites.

Let's hope such good ideas are contagious.

Simon Says
Bolivar

If you name something right, people are always giving you gifts. Name your son Percy, after your dad's rich uncle, and—aside from all the beatings he'll probably get on the playground—your rich relative will probably set the kid up with a trust fund that will have him laughing as he limps all the way to the bank. Name your boat Bud, and friends will never fail to bring a six-pack when they come aboard, acting as though it's a really witty joke nobody ever thought of before. Name your town Bolivar, and Venezuela will probably give you handsome statues of their revolutionary leader. It's happened to Bolivar, Missouri, twice now.

★ ★

I don't know if anybody has ever let it slip to the Venezuelans, but Bolivar is not actually named for Simón Bolívar. The town was named by settlers from Tennessee, and they just used the name of the town they came from (which *was* named for the South American freedom fighter).

But if a country wants to give you a handsome bronze statue of a take-charge-looking guy, you would be a fool to turn it down, even twice. So one Simón now stands in front of city hall, and the other, which came as a gift presented through President Harry S Truman, was erected at Neuhart Park on Albany Avenue. Do you think anybody in Venezuela would notice if they put a cowboy hat on one of these statues and named it for a former mayor?

One Tough Lady
Boonville

Boonville residents are proud to say they have a town mother, not a town father. And, sure enough, Hannah Cole (generally given credit for establishing Boonville) was quite a gal. Born in Wythe County, Virginia, in 1764, Hannah Allison and her younger sister, Phoebe, married brothers William and Stephen Cole. They all made their way west, by way of Kentucky, and during those years Hannah gave birth to nine children. By 1807 the two families had settled on Loutre Island, in the Missouri River, but in 1810 Hannah's husband was killed in an Indian raid. Later the same year, undaunted, Hannah Cole and her nine children, plus Stephen and Phoebe with their five, moved farther west and built homes south of the Missouri River near Franklin. This was the first white settlement south of the Missouri River in the new territory west of St. Louis.

During the War of 1812, hostilities broke out between the settlers and the Fox and Sac Native American tribes. Hannah fortified her cabin, which occupied a strategic high bluff, and armed it with a cannon. She held her ground. By the time a Christmas observance was recorded at her place in 1815, the outpost was being referred to as "Hannah Cole's fort." The "fort" served as both a military bastion and a field hospital, where Hannah cared for the sick, performed menial chores, and in "idle moments" cast lead bullets to arm against further attacks. She also bought and sold many acres of land in and around present-day Boonville and established the first local ferry service, operated by her sons. When her brother-in-law, Stephen Cole, helped organize Cooper County in 1818, Hannah Cole's fort was selected as the first county seat. Her cabin was one of four voting places used in the general election of 1819, and later it served as the first post office.

But when time came to plat and name the settlement surrounding Hannah Cole's fort, local organizers selected the name Boonville. In 1805 two sons of Daniel Boone had established a commercial salt lick across the river in Howard County, and the region had become known as Boone's Lick or Boonslick. Naming the new town for the famous Daniel Boone, who had also moved near his family's enterprise, simply made good business sense.

There is no indication that Hannah Cole disagreed, but if she was upset that the town wasn't named for her, she probably just went outside and killed a chicken. In 1825 Hannah built a new cabin near her son, Samuel, on land she owned south of Boonville. She moved there with a slave named Lucy and lived there for eighteen years, until her death in 1843 at the age of seventy-nine. Her grave lies in the Briscoe Cemetery, 12 miles south of Boonville, marked by a Daughters of the American Revolution memorial.

Will There Be an Intermission?

Boonville

Thespian Hall (522 Main Street) is a beautiful theater built in the Classical Greek Revival style. It is also the oldest theater west of the Allegheny Mountains that is still in use as a theater. There have been a few interruptions since the theater was completed in 1857, mind you. At various times Thespian Hall also served as a ballroom, an

★ ★

army barracks, a Civil War hospital, an armory, a Masonic hall, a skating rink, a gymnasium, an opera house, and a movie theater. Now it is the home of the Boonville Community Theater. I don't know about the actors, but it sounds as though there's hardly a role this theater hasn't played before.

Call Friends of Historic Boonville, who own the theater, for more information at (660) 882-7977.

Dueling with Dinosaurs
Camdenton

The Orion Science Center's mission statement declares, "Our goal is to create excitement in learning, encouraging visitors to seek to improve their minds and abilities and make them more productive and fulfilled people."

The center's Web site states that it is a "not for profit organization emphasizing conservative Christian influence on society." You won't hear a lot about Charles Darwin from these folks.

But Orion and its featured Dino Space Adventure Fun Park manage to combine really fun attractions with some controversial sides of learning and education debates. Parents may find themselves doing a little extra research to answer some of the questions kids come up with on the way home.

The Fun Park is geared to most children's need to burn off energy in active play. The adults who plan the exhibits also clearly recognize that kids have fears of unknown things, which tend to materialize in their minds as monsters. It is a short jump from monsters to dinosaurs, so by doing battle with dinosaurs in a playful educational setting, kids empower themselves and gain strength through learning.

Popular games and exhibits include Dinosaur Hunter, an anachronistic duel in which kid warriors are armed with a water sling called the Slingasaurus Destructis. In another educational anachronism, they take on more dinosaurs with a trebuchet, the catapult machine that was used to attack castles in the Middle Ages.

Without dinosaurs confronting them, kids can practice their skills with a bola, shoot water rockets, or just seesaw on a very clever adjustable teeter-totter. Then it's back to dinosaurs and their littler friends, as kids sift through the salted Fossil Pit, where they get to keep up to three of their "finds."

In the museum there's the Bone Room, with skeletons of both exotic and everyday creatures. The Puzzle Place is like a brainteaser you can get lost in, it is so much fun.

More games and exhibits are added periodically. That fact, plus the unpredictability of the interactions the kids dream up themselves, makes the Orion Science Center always fresh and new.

The Orion Science Center is located on MO 5, approximately 1.2 miles south of the US 54 intersection. Open March through October. Admission charged. For more information call (573) 346-5516 or visit www.dinospaceadventure.com.

Trivia

You have to crouch down to get a good look at the gravestone of Linnie Crouch, who died on April 26, 1826 (date of birth unknown). We don't even know anything about Linnie himself, except that his tiny tombstone appeared in *Ripley's Believe It or Not!* for being the world's smallest cemetery stone. Shaped like a book, the marker measures approximately 5 by 6 inches. A metal security rod also serves as a spine, allowing you to turn the stone "pages." There is no story inscribed therein, but the toughest critics will have to admit this is a novel way to mark a grave.

You'll find Linnie's little gravestone mounted on a board at ground level at the Oak Hill Cemetery in Butler, Missouri.

A Boon to Boonville in the Boondocks

Few people appreciate how big a step it was to establish paved roads as settlers moved westward. Prairie lands grew grasses so tall a rider on horseback could easily lose his or her way in summer. When the rich land was wet, the passing of just a few wagons along a trail could turn the track into a deep mire that might be impassable for weeks. In central Missouri land that was not prairie was a mass of thick forest broken only by rivers and swamps.

For the first few decades of exploration, most settlers made their way west along the river corridors. Little villages and forts along the rivers gave the new immigrants a foothold on the land, and from there they gradually penetrated the interior.

Because Boonville occupied the higher ground, it survived while its big-sister city, Franklin, was swept away in a succession of floods. Yet cargo delivered by riverboats to Boonville still had to somehow be transported up the high bluffs in a land virtually devoid of stone. Even surefooted mules could not pull much weight up the tall soil embankments, especially when they were wet.

A solution was found in the ballast stones that boats traveling upstream needed when their cargo was light. Arriving at a destination like Boonville, the river boatmen would cast their ballast stones ashore in order to load up with commodities like pork, flour, and tobacco to be taken downstream. Over time, huge piles of river-polished cobblestones accumulated, providing material for Boonville's first paved road.

Said to be the first paved road west of St. Louis, the unmortared limestone cobblestones leading up "Wharf Hill" were fitted tightly between cut limestone curbs spaced 50 feet apart. To prevent the road's washing out, cobblestone drainage ditches were fashioned alongside. The city's first modern thoroughfare was created, and on it commerce could continue in almost any weather.

By the end of the 1860s, the railroad had reached Boonville, and other cargo depots replaced the river landing at Wharf Hill. The north end of the street was eventually covered by 3 to 4 feet of soil, and in 1924 the Old Trails National Highway Bridge across the Missouri cut into the south end of the cobblestone street.

In 1989, during the construction of a new river bridge, the forgotten cobblestone street was discovered under what had become US 40. Town leaders recognized the significance of what some might have bulldozed away as just a nuisance pile of rubble. A portion of the cobblestone street was restored, a city park with an interpretive trail was created, and a significant landmark in Missouri's history was saved.

Wharf Hill might not be anything you'd want to take your skateboard down today, but believe me, they thought it was a sweet street back then.

Skateboarders won't bother you here.
JULIUS UDINYIWE, HOPE PHOTO

★ ★

No Laughing Matter
Camdenton

Ha Ha Tonka might sound like a funny place, but it seems as though the land was a jinx to previous owners.

Robert M. Snyder, a wealthy Kansas City businessman, bought more than 5,000 acres here in the early 1900s, where he began building a sixty-room, European-style castle. Just a year later, in 1906, he was killed in one of the state's first automobile accidents. His sons tried to complete their father's project, but financial problems caused

Some castles just weren't meant to be.
MISSOURI DIVISION OF TOURISM

them to scale back the original plans, and subsequently the building was leased as a hotel.

In 1942 sparks from a chimney ignited the roof, and the entire interior was gutted by fire. In 1976 vandals burned the 80-foot water tower. Now all that remains of the grand mansion are the spooky yet beautiful castle walls, looking for all the world like the setting for a Scottish romance novel.

Ha Ha Tonka is worth a visit for other reasons besides the castle ruins. The property, now a state park, is a showcase of Missouri's karst topography—a honeycomb of caverns, sinkholes, springs, over-hangs, and natural bridges. Bluffs 250 feet high rise above Ha Ha Tonka Spring, which discharges about forty-eight million gallons of water each day. Aboveground, Ha Ha Tonka Savanna Natural Area displays one of the state's best examples of this landscape, which is not quite forest, not quite prairie.

Exploring the many lovely self-guided or ranger-guided trails, you get the impression that Robert Snyder and his family might have been spared their strange fate if he hadn't attempted to improve upon the beauty of this place.

The park is free and open year-round and is located 5 miles southwest of Camdenton off US 54. Visit www.mostateparks.com/hahatonka.htm or call (573) 346-2986.

Vennard's Dinosaur Sculptures
Centralia

Larry Vennard is a funny guy. But his sense of humor is visual rather than verbal and sometimes very subtle. This journeyman welder lives on T Highway in Audrain County, not far from Centralia, so when he wanted a signature sculpture for his front yard, he made a T. rex. The towering sculpture is now surrounded by a bunch of other dinosaurs, plus two warriors attacking the beast with arrows and spears. The ferocity of the scene is tempered by a family of sparrows nesting just above one of the T. rex's claws. Over closer to the house, an army of

★ ★

metal mosquitoes flies in formation, gently buffeted by breezes. Caterpillars climb trees and march across the lawn. A 3-foot spider seems to look for a place to spin her web, as equally large dragonflies perch nearby. Almost all Vennard's artistic creations are of living things, real or imagined. The challenge he seems to love is breathing life into cold pieces of inanimate iron.

Originally from Iowa, Vennard learned his welding trade in the oil fields out west. He soon mastered "making things straight," but he kept feeling the higher calling to make art with his tools. Pieces of iron lying about would remind him of a head, a body, or a wing. He just couldn't rest until he had put the whole creature together. After an automobile accident almost killed him in 1993, doctors told Vennard he would have to give up welding entirely. He stubbornly insisted that he could still do art welding with scrap metal, and the pleasure he found in that seemed to give him confidence that he could also resume commercial welding. Vennard gradually got back to doing "ordinary" welding jobs for local farmers and whomever else needed him, but the number of sculptures in his yard continues to grow.

People are beginning to make pilgrimages out to see his work, and some good commissions have followed. Vennard can sometimes be coaxed to sell a piece directly out of his yard, but he is more apt to say he'll build you a little better one than that, with what he learned from making the first one. Because of their size, several of Vennard's most remarkable pieces are rarely seen off the farm. "But when we load them up and take them somewhere," he grins, "you ought to see those other drivers' expressions!"

To please Vennard by gawking at the sculptures in his yard, take Jefferson Street north from Centralia to where it becomes Highway C. Continue north to Highway T on your right. Drive about 2.5 miles; start looking right and you'll see all kinds of reasons to smile.

Call (573) 682-5908 if you would like an appointment.

T. rex never gets off the farm.

★ ★

Beetle Bailey Back at School
Columbia

Beetle Bailey became famous as the lazy U.S. Army private who constantly sought to shirk work and outsmart his goofy sergeant. But in addition to making cartoonist Mort Walker famous and wealthy, Beetle Bailey committed one particular act of integrity and bravery that still deserves commendation today.

Clear back in the early 1950s, Mort Walker established himself as a bit of an independent thinker and realist, even as he sought to portray army life through the medium of a newspaper cartoon. The Tokyo edition of the military newspaper *Stars and Stripes* dropped the cartoon because some of the pompous military brass believed the strip caused disrespect toward officers among enlisted men.

Newspapers back in the States had a field day with that story. *Stars and Stripes* eventually capitulated, and circulation stateside jumped by one hundred newspapers.

But it was in 1970, when Walker introduced the character of Lt. Jack Flap, a black officer, that courage and values were tested. Several Southern newspapers dropped the cartoon strip, but during the ensuing publicity, another one hundred papers picked up *Beetle Bailey* in support of the nation's first integrated cartoon strip.

In 2000 the U.S. Army awarded Walker the Decoration for Distinguished Civilian Service in a ceremony at the Pentagon. Bestowing its highest civilian honor on Walker, the military acknowledged his role in boosting troop morale and advocating civil rights within the armed services.

Walker also created the cartoon strip *Hi and Lois,* spun off when Beetle went on leave and visited his sister, Lois, back in 1954. Two other strips, *Boner's Ark* and *Sam & Silo,* testify to Mort Walker's legendary creativity, energy, and drive. In 1974 he created the (now International) Museum of Cartoon Art, located in Boca Raton, Florida, and in 1989 he was inducted into the Cartoon Art Hall of Fame.

In 1992 Walker, a University of Missouri graduate under the G.I.

Private Bailey never budges from his favorite booth.
MU PUBLICATIONS AND ALUMNI COMMUNICATIONS

Bill, presented the campus with a life-size statue of Beetle Bailey seated at a table representing a booth at the Shack, a local college hangout that burned down in 1988. From there Beetle can leisurely watch as the busy life on campus passes by. In the spirit of the cartoon strip, in which Walker often placed graffiti making references to college pals, the statue contains similar carved names and initials and sentiments. Alumni donors contributed 50 percent of the statue's cost and in return got to have their sentiments etched into the table as graffiti. The other 50 percent of the statue's cost was contributed by Walker and King Syndicates.

To get a sense of where some of Walker's early ideas formed and fomented, stop by and take a seat next to Beetle Bailey outside the Alumni Center on Conley Avenue on the university campus. Maybe an urge to get back to work will overtake you.

Making Pneumatic New Again
Columbia

Back in the 1950s quite a few offices and department stores still used pneumatic tubes to send messages and small packets zipping around with strong blasts of air. Today about the only common use of this form of conveyance is at drive-up bank windows. If a University of Missouri professor has his way, this will one day change.

Professor Henry Liu has been researching the potential of sending coal over long distances via something called "capsule pipeline transport." CPT, or "underground freight transport," as it is sometimes called, has the potential to move a vast array of commodities efficiently over long distances in a manner that would be less susceptible to severe weather or terrorist attacks.

Japan uses a similar system to move earth-filled capsules on wheels for a few miles using forced air. Professor Liu's research, supported by state and federal sources, sends "logs" of compressed coal through a 1,400-foot water-filled pipeline out behind the university's Dairy Barn. Commercial applications could be just a year or two away.

According to Liu, pipe is cheaper to lay than rail. The fact that such transport is both automatic and secure is another key factor recommending this technology. Estimates are that an efficient underground transport system could replace 5 to 10 percent of rail traffic and almost 70 percent of commercial trucking. Obstacles include resistance from traditional transportation industries, issues of eminent domain, and high-tech industries that wish to divert investment elsewhere.

So don't look for 18-wheelers to disappear from the highways anytime soon.

The Showing Is Over
Columbia

Willard Duncan Vandiver—the man credited with coming up with the often-repeated statement "I'm from Missouri, you've got to show me"—ironically wasn't originally from Missouri at all. Born near Moorefield in Hardy County, Virginia, on March 30, 1854, Vandiver moved with his parents three years later to a farm in Boone County, Missouri.

Vandiver studied law but graduated to teach natural sciences and eventually became president of the state normal school in Cape Girardeau. Active in Democratic Party politics, in 1897 he was elected to the first of four consecutive terms in the U.S. House of Representatives. It was reportedly there, when in a crucial debate, that he expressed his skepticism for something a fellow congressman had said by uttering the famous line. By then Vandiver's birthplace had become part of West Virginia, so to be completely accurate, he would have had to say something like "I'm from Virginia, but my family moved to Missouri when I was just a lad. After that, part of Virginia became West Virginia in a political compromise; therefore I'm not really sure where I'm from, so you've got to show me."

Doesn't have quite the same resonance, does it?

Well it's a moot point now, because Vandiver died in 1932 and was buried in Columbia Cemetery. Nobody is going to show him anything anymore. Still, we can thank him for our state nickname, wherever you want to say he is from.

Delicate Work with Scrap Iron
Concordia

Wendell Olson is a modest man. He wasn't available when I went by to admire his yard art, and when I called back later to discuss his creations, he seemed surprised by the attention. He said he is pleased people seem to enjoy his work, but he seldom sells one of his pieces.

★ ★

A fish, barely caught, is bearly fried in Concordia.

I gathered that when he does, it is usually donated for a local charity.

Wendell's sculptures are, unlike their creator, boisterous and a bit silly. He began making them, he told me, after he had a bit of heart trouble and wanted something to do. His two self-imposed rules are first, all works must be made with just basic hand tools, and second, most of the materials should be rusty and cheap.

In his yard, along the road, you might first spy his pair of coiled wire bears fishing for salmon. A tin man stands guard off to one side, while a crocodile lies in wait on the grass. A giant slice of watermelon gives bright color to the background of his chaotic outside art display, yet several impressive arrangements of giant plants and flowers bloom only in muted tones of tin and rust.

I marveled at Wendell's sturdy locomotive train and a separate comical caboose. There's a whimsical space ship, a turtlelike tank, and a Dutch-style windmill too. But when asked, Olson said his proudest accomplishment is his large Ford tri-motor wind vane, about 15 feet long, mounted on a stand in such a way that it appears to be banking gently in flight.

If you have a ton of old scrap iron lying around, you might give it to Wendell Olson. The artist has a light touch.

Take exit 58 off I-70 and drive on MO 23 toward Concordia. Turn right onto North Main, then left onto Northeast Second. Finally, turn left to 201 North Golden Award Drive.

"Fan" Cliburn tickles the iron keys in Concordia.

History in Pictures
Jefferson City

Larger-than-life men and women with angular features and muscular limbs toil, play, and live out their famous lives before your eyes at the Missouri State Capitol building. Looking at the various panels of the mural, you get the sense that even the anonymous people played a significant role in shaping this state. They are part of Thomas Hart Benton's *The Social History of the State of Missouri,* a mural that teaches visitors much about Missouri history and doesn't shy away from difficult subjects.

Completed in 1936, the painting is very much in the style of Depression-era art, with which Benton has become so closely associated. In the populist spirit that gripped America at that time, Benton let the public view him at work during the two years he was painting. A small note was posted, requesting that visitors refrain from making suggestions. Although there were often hostile outcries, there's no record that the artist let the hubbub slow him down. After the mural was completed, Benton frequently said it was his favorite painting.

"Pioneer Days" is perhaps the least controversial panel, depicting Mark Twain's characters Huckleberry Finn and Jim on their voyage down the Mississippi; settlers clearing the land and felling forests; and, in one corner, men trading whiskey to the Indians. This latter unflattering depiction bothers many people, for different reasons, still. The "Politics, Farming, and Law in Missouri" panel shows as much about civil strife and lawlessness as it does about the nobler aspects of these terms, with the Civil War itself represented by a dark column of smoke against which are depictions of slavery and a lynching. Then there's the "St. Louis and Kansas City" panel, a sprawling portrayal of the "shoes and booze" reputation of St. Louis, along with a scene of the tragic love triangle made famous in the blues song "Frankie and Johnny." As if to avoid picking favorites, Kansas City is represented with unvarnished looks at railroads, stockyards, and a meeting with Boss Tom Pendergast.

Perhaps because it succeeded in offending so many people on different sides of various issues, Benton's mural survived the initial protests when it was officially unveiled. But the painting almost did not survive the warm, humid conditions in the building or visitors' continual testing of the paint with fingernails and pocketknives. In 1960 Benton hired his friend and colleague, Sidney Larson, to restore *The Social History of the State of Missouri* under his direction. Immediately afterward, humidity and temperature controls were put in place to ensure a long-lasting run. With each passing year, more of the controversy seems to fade and Missourians seem to take pride in this unique and beautiful painting. Hopefully it will never fail to stir emotions within those who view it or educate us all to the colorful history of the Show Me State.

For more information call (573) 751-2854 or visit www.mostate parks.com/statecapcomplex.

You're Going to Put That Thing Where?

Jefferson City

According to the Missouri Veterinary Medical Association, there's only one place in the United States where you can visit a museum dedicated exclusively to veterinary medicine. It's hard to imagine what else might fit in with this theme, which has brought together 3,500 artifacts (at last count) in the Jefferson City Museum. Maybe all the other cow hairballs and pig kidney stones are in private collections.

In any event, a tour through the Veterinary Museum will be a real eye-opener and will keep your eleven-year-old discussing disgusting things he learned about for weeks (usually during dinner).

Instruments dating back several centuries were once used to poke, prod, puncture, and immobilize all manner of beasts for their good health. Usually it was difficult to convince the dog, cat, cow, horse, mule, chicken, or pig that the necessary therapy was for its own good, hence there are numerous instruments that were used to sedate the animals and more equipment to immobilize them even further.

An exceedingly rare display is a steamer trunk filled with all the instruments a late nineteenth-century horse doctor would use to treat horses and mules. (That would have been the rough equivalent of an automobile engine repair shop today.)

There are manuscripts filled with the wisdom and strange notions of how to maintain animal health. You'll learn what was used to catch hogs, what a wooden balling gun was used for, and why a

Amazing tools to retrieve unbelievable objects from the strangest places.
KIM C. RALSTON, MISSOURI VETERINARY MEDICAL FOUNDATION

veterinarian would want to puncture an animal's stomach with a Swiss trocar. But most appealing to the young and young at heart are the slightly gross and yucky bones, animal skins, embryos, and stomach contents revealed by this singular collection.

The artifacts are presented well, in an educational context, so what may draw some in with morbid curiosity will cause them to leave with a new respect for the profession of veterinary medicine and the measures it has taken over the years to preserve the health of our animal friends.

The museum is open Wednesday through Friday from noon to 4:00 p.m. and Saturday by appointment. It is located at 2500 Country Club Drive. To get there take US 50 west to MO 179. When you exit, turn right; Country Club Drive will be your first right. Watch for the museum on your left. Call (573) 636-8737 for more information.

A Puzzlement

Lebanon

I don't understand. If you were going to "retire," would you start a business with a huge inventory beside a busy highway and work long hours seven days a week, fifty weeks a year? Then, in your "spare" time, would you take up a woodworking craft requiring skill, patience, steady hands, and sharp eyes?

That's exactly what Nancy Ballhagen and her husband did when they started Nancy Ballhagen's Puzzles. Located just a stone's throw across I-44 from Old Route 66, outside Lebanon near Sleeper Junction, this is a store you have to see to believe. They have 2,400 different puzzles in stock, some of which have more than 13,000 pieces. They've got die-cut, cork-backed, metallic, wooden, 3-D, lighted, clock, calendar, and hologram puzzles (to name a few). They have puzzles in styles called "cyberealism" and "photomosaic." They have the world's smallest puzzles and some of the world's largest.

The inventory is organized by artist, theme, style, country, age group, and other ways I couldn't begin to figure out. Then, to top it

Granny Nanny hand-cuts a puzzle.
KEITH BALLHAGEN

all off, Nancy makes wonderful wooden puzzles under the name "Granny Nanny." These intricate puzzles are signed and dated by Nancy, usually with figure pieces that match the theme of the overall puzzle. Thus her dragon-and-castle puzzle has pieces shaped like unicorns and other things magical. Her Route 66 puzzle has pieces shaped like cars and trucks. Noah's Ark puzzle has . . . yup, you guessed it. These would make great Christmas gifts, but don't wait until Christmas morning. Christmas and Thanksgiving used to be just about the only days Nancy Ballhagen's puzzle store was closed, but Nancy has had to cut way back. You can look as you drive by on I-44 to see if she is open. If she is, take exit 135 off I-44 east of Lebanon and follow the outer road east 0.75 mile. Otherwise visit www.missouripuzzle.com or call (417) 286-3837.

Ka-ka-ka-Katy!

I guess you could say Katy Trail State Park is the biggest little park, or the littlest big park, in the country. Officially it is the longest Rails to Trails state park in the United States, stretching more than 225 miles from Clinton to St. Charles. First formed in 1986 when the Missouri-Kansas-Texas Railroad (Katy, for short) ceased operation of its Machens to Sedalia line, the trail was made possible by the National Trails System Act. That federal legislation provides a means by which unused railroad corridors are "banked" for possible future transportation needs but are kept open as thoroughfares for hikers and bikers, as well as other outdoor enthusiasts.

In 1991 the Katy Trail was extended by the addition of 33 miles ceded by the Union Pacific Railroad from its line between Sedalia and Clinton. As long as the Katy Trail is—stretching for many miles along the Missouri River and through some of the most beautiful countryside in the state—in most parts the trail is so narrow a child could throw a ball across its width.

For more information visit www.mostateparks.com or call (800) 334-6946.

The Katy Trail parallels the Missouri River for much of its length.

Rock around the Clock

Lincoln

Every September for more than forty years, several hundred devoted rock fans have gathered in Lincoln to get a little crazy and do their thing. When these people get stoned, though, they are passing around amazing stuff like mozarkite, double terminator quartz, greenstone, and lapidary supplies.

You have stumbled onto the Mozarkite Society's Rock, Mineral and Jewelry Show, a three-day event of mineral fanatics that includes the ongoing rock swap and craft show, camping (if you want to), silent auctions, a big dinner, live music, and lots and lots of rock.

Mozarkite makes it official that Missouri really rocks.
MOZARKITE SOCIETY OF LINCOLN, INC.

Lincoln is the mozarkite capital of the world, and mozarkite is the state rock of Missouri. Benton County has the best deposits of the green, red, and purple semiprecious stone in the state, so rock hounds, crafters, and jewelry buffs from all over come here to get their fair share. People from elsewhere bring what they have to sell and swap, so when everybody gets together, you've got a rock extravaganza.

Lincoln Community Park, where this all happens during the third full weekend in September, is one of the largest multiuse parks you'll find in any small town. Lincoln is on US 65, south of Sedalia and north of Warsaw. For more information call Jean Eckstein at (660) 668-2752. To arrange to dig for mozarkite locally during the rest of the year, contact Linville Harms at (660) 827-4143.

Rock on!

Doggone Wonderful

Marshall

People say that poor ole Jim was such a homely Llewellyn setter that Sam Van Arsdale bought the pup for a measly $5, one-fifth the price paid for his litter mates. Van Arsdale, an avid hunter who spent a lot of time and money training his young dogs, found Jim to be lazy, repeatedly refusing to participate in puppy practice routines. He nearly gave the pup away, but when he finally coaxed Jim to accompany him on his first hunt, the untrained dog quickly pointed to a covey of quail.

Later Van Arsdale said, "Jim, let's find a hickory tree to sit under and rest awhile," and the dog dutifully trotted ahead and sat under a hickory. Mocking that seeming coincidence, Sam said, "Well, if you're so smart, show me a pin oak." Jim did. (And there are a lot of humans who couldn't do that.) That same day, the dog correctly identified several more trees and shrubs.

Once, when a stray pregnant cat turned up, Van Arsdale put ten slips of paper in front of Jim, five marked MALE, and five marked FEMALE. He asked his dog to predict the litter, which Jim did perfectly—two males and three females. Jim also accurately predicted

★ ★

the gender of six human babies, until Van Arsdale stopped allowing human birth predictions.

One night in the Sedalia hotel Sam owned at the time, some of Van Arsdale's friends were talking about the Kentucky Derby. The men wanted to know if Jim could predict the winner. Van Arsdale wrote the names of all the horses on slips of paper and sealed each one in an envelope. He then passed the slips around so that no one knew who held which name. Jim was asked to go to the man who had the name of the horse that would win. Jim followed instructions, and the selected envelope, still sealed, was locked in a safe. After the Derby, the envelope was opened—it held the winning horse's name. In a similar fashion Jim picked six more Derby winners in a row. Other experiments were conducted that seemed to demonstrate that "Jim the Wonder Dog" could understand French, German, Spanish, Greek, shorthand, and Morse code. Professors from Washington University and the University of Missouri at Columbia examined Jim and tested him, afterward declaring they could find no explanation other than the dog possessed psychic powers.

In 1933 Jim was invited to a joint session of the Missouri legislature. Although he did not know the men assembled there, when asked to find the man named Beau Brummel, Jim did so. Knowing Van Arsdale did not know Morse code, someone had the state telegrapher come in and tap out another legislator's name. Jim trotted to the rear of the chamber, edged down a row, and put his paw on the correct man's knee. Jim performed several other amazing feats for the dumbfounded legislators that day.

Although dogs are usually colorblind, Jim could find people when they were described by the color of clothing they were wearing. He also could correctly pick out people described by a phrase, such as "tall and handsome." When asked to find a Bible, Jim went to a minister in the crowd who had one in his pocket, and when asked who a person could go to with a stomachache, he went to a doctor he had never seen before.

Sam Van Arsdale refused a one-year "six-figure" Hollywood

contract for his dog, saying that while he did not understand Jim's gifts, he didn't want to commercialize his dog. He did, however, allow other public appearances before Jim's death from a heart attack while on a fishing trip with Sam in 1937. By then Van Arsdale owned a hotel in Marshall, Missouri. Jim was refused burial in the family plot inside the cemetery because he was a dog, so his grave and a marker were placed just outside, where it still receives more visitors than the humans buried inside the gates.

In 1999 the city of Marshall dedicated a memorial park to Jim the Wonder Dog. It is on the square, at the site formerly occupied by Van Arsdale's hotel. The Marshall Ridge Park Cemetery gate where Jim was buried is off MO 41, north of Sedalia in Saline County.

Shocking Medical Practice

Nevada

Dr. J. T. Hornback graduated from medical school in Kansas City just before 1900 and set up practice in downtown Nevada after marrying Geordia Munn, a local girl. In 1908 Dr. Hornback put a state-of-the-art doctor's office in the basement of a new addition onto the family home. He practiced there for almost twenty years, and when he suffered a debilitating stroke and later died, no one in the family disturbed his things.

Mrs. Hornback and then her daughter, Helene, continued to live in the home until 1993. Three years later the Hornbacks' son, Hope, a Harvard-educated mathematician, donated the home and all of its contents to the Historical Society. Several rooms of the Hornback home are now on permanent display in the Bushwhacker Museum, but the most unusual is Dr. Hornback's office. The good doctor was something of a technology wonk in his day—he was one of the first doctors in Nevada to use an X-ray machine—and he stayed current on other diagnostic and treatment methods. (The museum's staff had considerable difficulty discovering how to safely dispose of the contents of many of Dr. Hornback's medicine bottles, considered environmental hazards and poisons today.)

★ ★

But the most fun feature of this physician's arsenal is a rare 1905 Wagner Mica-Plate Electrostatic Machine. The device is a huge piece of beautifully constructed furniture, with glass sides surrounding a large mica-sided drum. A hand crank turns the drum, generating static electricity, which was sent coursing through patients' bodies in attempts to cure everything from migraines to infections. Sadly there is no evidence that this treatment ever cured anybody, but everyone definitely got a charge out of it.

If this sparks your curiosity, you can visit the Bushwhacker Museum, located in the basement of the Nevada Public Library at 231 North Main Street. The museum is open Monday through Saturday, May through October. Call (417) 667-7108 or visit www.bushwhacker.org for details.

The Tin Men
Nevada

In 1978 Robert Quitno bought the W. F. Norman Corporation, a company that made relatively boring things like shower stalls and metal boxes. It was a little dull, but a going concern. Deep within his company's storage spaces, Robert found plaster-of-paris molds, iron dies, antique drop hammers, and other machine-tool equipment that had been used to turn out ornate tin ceiling panels more than half a century before. In the late 1800s and the early 1900s, pressed tin largely replaced plaster and lath as an inexpensive "counterfeit" of more expensive hand-carved plaster ceilings. Metal ceilings had the additional advantage of being fireproof, and they remained in vogue until the Great Depression halted most construction. World War II diverted peacetime metal manufacturing to more critical needs, and when postwar construction began, other materials were being used for ceilings and trim.

Quitno didn't know much about the tin ceiling panels he found, but he showed some to a Kansas City architect, who got very excited. At the time, people who were restoring early twentieth-century buildings could only get replacement tin ceilings by salvaging them from other old buildings. And the nostalgia craze was only just getting under way. So Robert retooled with the old equipment and began pounding out tin ceiling panels again. Where once there had been about two dozen companies manufacturing such tin ceilings, after a fifty-year hiatus, Quitno's operation was now virtually the only one. Business boomed. The family bought another company and added outdoor architectural ornaments, most notably gargoyles, to their line.

Robert has passed on, but his family continues with the business. In addition to the architectural trade, they are now doing a brisk business with Hollywood and television studios. If you keep your eye peeled, you may see W. F. Norman ceilings and architectural ornaments in the sets of *Spider-Man,* the *Law and Order* courtroom, *Cinderella Man, Home Alone 2, Maverick,* and *Malcolm X,* as well as the studio set for Conan O'Brien. Recently they made replacement urns for the Henry Ford Museum. You can also see W. F. Norman ceilings at Ford's Theatre in Washington, D.C., and Pickfair, the Hollywood home of Mary Pickford and Douglas Fairbanks.

The W. F. Norman Corporation is located at 214 North Cedar Street in Nevada. Customers and persons inquiring about special jobs can view the operation by appointment or request more information by calling (417) 667-5552 or visiting www.wfnorman.com.

Open Wide

Rich Hill

People insist on calling Big Mouth a coal shovel when she is, in fact, more properly called a bucket. Whatever you want to call her (and I hasten to point out that the designation of monstrous Big Mouth as feminine was not mine), she is huge.

The Pittsburg & Midway Coal Company donated the bucket to the city of Rich Hill in honor of the community's significant contribution to the coal mining industry. Big Mouth served her tour of duty attached to the Midway Princess, an equally grand-scale dragline that was used to remove overburden (dirt and rocks) that lay over the rich coal deposits being sought below. Once the coal seam was revealed, front-end loaders were used to extract the coal and dump it into trucks.

★ ★

To appreciate the size of Big Mouth, you really have to stop by Rich Hill City Park and gape. Your jaw will drop open when you realize one of those dump trucks that removed the coal could be parked inside Big Mouth. Every Christmas the Coalminers' Daughters, a local women's civic organization, places a life-size Nativity scene within the bucket's protective shelter.

One scoop by Big Mouth could dig to a depth of 125 feet. That single fill could measure more than seventy cubic yards and weigh as much as forty to forty-four tons.

Big Mouth's bucket is big enough to shelter
a life-size Nativity scene.

The Midway Princess was disassembled in the early 1990s and sent to duty in the York Canyon Mine near Raton, New Mexico. But Big Mouth will remain at Rich Hill permanently, telling a proud story of her coal mining past.

Rich Hill is approximately 20 miles north of Nevada on U.S. 71. Big Mouth is situated in the city park, diagonally across the parking lot from City Hall.

Carnivores' Cavern
Richland

Back during Prohibition, a cave outside Richland was the hottest entertainment spot for miles around, where liquor flowed and flappers danced the Charleston. When drinking alcoholic beverages was legal again, people didn't have to sneak out to the remote cave in a cliff 100 feet above the Gasconade River to sip spirits or cut a rug. When David Hughes bought the property, it was hard to believe that the cave had ever housed so much fun and frivolity.

For one thing, the cave's floor was covered with 2 feet of pigeon droppings. But when neighbors told Hughes stories of how popular the cave had once been, the retired farmer and welder got an idea. He spent five years carefully enlarging the cave, jackhammering ledges and removing 2,000 tons of rock. The result became Caveman Bar-BQ & Steak House, one of the most remarkable barbecue restaurants in Missouri. In 2009 the enterprise was purchased by popular Lebanon, Missouri, restaurateur Gary Dyer, who has renamed it the Cave Restaurant.

A couple of water pools add ambience and also provide a place for the nine pounds of water removed from the otherwise humid air every hour. The pools contain fish, but you'll never notice everything on a first visit. The restaurant is smoke free and can seat 225 diners at once. With little restaurant competition in the area, even above-ground, the unique setting and popular menu keep the place filled to capacity, especially on weekends.

The restaurant's menu includes Italian entrees, steaks, seafood, and chicken, plus a celebrated Jack Daniels bread pudding. For added

★ ★

ambience, the Cave annually celebrates the Enchanted Cave Christmas. Cavemen never had it so good.

Near mile marker 150 of I-44, between St. Louis and Springfield, take the State Route W exit toward Richland. A small sign directs you to a parking lot, where you will be transported to the elevator that opens out into the cave. Open Wednesday through Sunday year-round, except in inclement weather. Reservations are required for groups of twenty or more. Anticipate a wait on weekends. For more information call (573) 765-4554 or visit www.thecave restaurantandresort.com.

Here's your chance to eat where flappers once partied and bats once flapped.
MISSOURI DIVISION OF TOURISM

✯ ✯

Did You Say "Peanut Butter"?

Sedalia

I know it sounds awful, but the signature entree at the old-fashioned, 1950s-style Wheel Inn Drive-In is a hamburger grilled with peanut butter, then served up with tomato, lettuce, pickles, and mayonnaise. You might order your first Guberburger just to gross out your friends, but after one taste you'll probably be back for more. These weird-sounding burgers have pleased generations of customers, and the fact that the Wheel Inn has for years been just across from the state fairgrounds has helped spread the Guberburger's fame.

Wheel on into the Wheel Inn for a taste of the original Guberburger.

So spread on the peanut butter and fire up the grill. I'll be in a jam if I don't get one soon!

The Wheel Inn Drive-In is located at 2103 North Limit Avenue in Sedalia, along US 65 by the state fairgrounds. Open daily 10:00 a.m. to 9:00 p.m. Call (660) 826-5177.

Just a Simple Country Lawyer
Sedalia

You can't drive north of Sedalia on US 65 without noticing the big stone castle perched in the woods on a 120-foot bluff. Built in stages from 1897 to 1928, the thirty-one-room, 12,000-square-foot castle was the little getaway place of Sedalia attorney and politician John Homer Bothwell. It was constructed with native limestone in the Arts and Crafts style so popular at the turn of the twentieth century, resulting in both the castle and its furnishings possessing a pleasant, casual feel appropriate to a rich man's country retreat. In addition, the handsome structure was built atop three natural caves in an early attempt to moderate the home's temperature, much like modern heat pumps.

As one might guess from the ambitious scale and high profile of the home he called Stonyridge Farm, Bothwell was a wheeler-dealer to be reckoned with in the state legislature. Many of his deals are little known today, but his influence was critical in the decision to permanently locate the Missouri State Fair in Sedalia, bringing with it plenty of revenue. He represented Pettis County for a total of sixteen years in the General Assembly and made one, unsuccessful run for governor in 1904.

Bothwell State Historic Site offers tours of the castle daily March through October and Thursday through Sunday November through February. The grounds offer beautiful trails with spectacular views, lovely picnic areas, and a children's playground.

The park is located at 19349 Bothwell Park Road, east of US 65, north of Sedalia. If you are headed north, watch for a small sign on your right just about the time you finish gawking at the castle. If you are headed south, take the first road on your left as soon as you see the castle (you won't have time to gawk).

Old Drum Resounds around the World

Warrensburg

Back in 1870, Leonidas Hornsby had been losing sheep to marauding dogs and swore that he would shoot the next dog that came onto his property. When that hapless dog turned out to be Old Drum, a hound that belonged to his brother-in-law—a hound Hornsby had hunted with and complimented—it made no difference. He had his nephew and ward, Samuel "Dick" Ferguson, shoot Old Drum, and the deed was done—but not forgotten.

Charles Burden, Old Drum's owner, sued Hornsby in a bitter legal dispute that eventually went all the way to the Missouri Supreme Court. No fewer than five prominent attorneys took part in the case, but the most famous and winning argument was delivered by future senator George Graham Vest. His eloquence has caused some to believe that his final summation is the origin of the expression "man's best friend," although there is no evidence he uttered those precise words.

What does survive is approximately the first half of Vest's speech, now known as the "Eulogy to the Dog," which would bring a tear to the eye of even the most dog-despising cat lady. Vest said, in part, "The one absolutely unselfish friend that a man can have in this selfish world, the one that never deserts him and the one that never proves ungrateful or treacherous is his dog. . . . When the last scene of all comes, and death takes the master in its embrace and his body is laid away in the cold ground, no matter if all other friends pursue their way, there by his graveside will the noble dog be found, his head between his paws, his eyes sad but open in alert watchfulness, faithful and true even to death."

We were robbed of the chance to know if Old Drum would have been so loyal to his master in death, but thanks to Senator Vest's speechifying, Leonidas Hornsby was ordered to pay his brother-in-law the grand sum of $50. The jury took only a few minutes to decide. Dick Ferguson later moved to Oklahoma, where he, himself, was shot and killed.

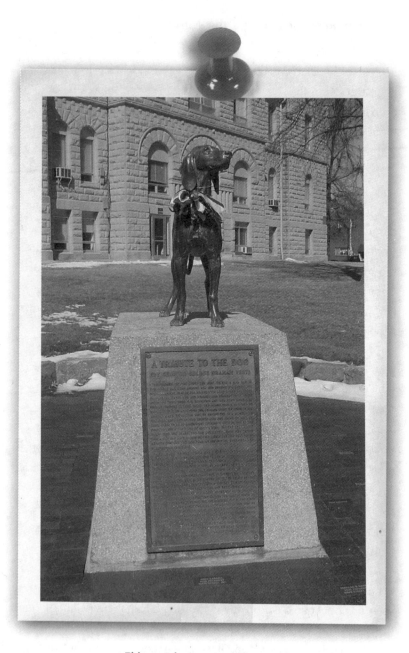

This pooch prompted the world's most famous
speech about a dog, man's best friend.

★ ★

In 1958 a statue of Old Drum was placed on the Johnson County Courthouse lawn in Warrensburg to serve as a memorial and to commemorate one of the greatest courtroom speeches ever delivered. You will be amazed to sit and watch how every few minutes people come by to snap a photo or to just gaze quietly into Old Drum's eyes. Doubtless many of them are dog lovers, but the day I was there I swear more than half of them were lawyers.

A client as good as Old Drum only comes along once in a lifetime.

Warrensburg is at the intersection of MO 13 and US 50. Proceed to the downtown square, where you will find Old Drum patiently waiting for you.

A Little Box Store

Williamsburg

Crane's Country Store has served the tiny town of Williamsburg in Calloway County since 1926. Owner David Crane is the fourth generation of his family to serve the community from the old-fashioned general store that is still heated with a woodstove in cold weather.

Locals and employees from the nearby Calloway Nuclear Plant make up most of his clientele, but some people drive long distances to visit a general store like they remember from their childhood.

Crane's is the kind of place that carries a little bit of everything, so customers stopping in for bread might discover a good deal on work boots. Also popular are Crane's dollar-deal sandwiches: "one meat, one cheese, one dollar."

David's mom and dad, Marlene and Joe, run a museum largely stocked with equipment and merchandise Crane's used to use and sell. There are wonderful old toys, and you can get a nostalgic peek at what a small-town White Eagle Gas Station looked like before the big box stores and galloping gas stations came to dominate America.

Take the Williamsburg exit (161) off I-70. Why don't you splurge and order a second meat and cheese? For more information call (866) 254-3311.

Something Fishy

There must have been a considerable row back in 1997 when the Missouri legislature met to select a state fish. The channel catfish won that title, but in a strange compromise, the American (Mississippi) paddlefish (*Polyodon spathula*) became Missouri's official state aquatic animal. Paddlefish, or spoonbill catfish as they are sometimes called, have also been called "freshwater sharks," because they have no bony skeleton, and "freshwater whales," because they skim plankton for food. Descended from prehistoric ancestors that swam 300 to 400 million years ago, these fish really look the part.

Shark-gray in color, they appear to be mostly belly and maw, with a long, flat, serrated snout extending out like a swordfish's sword. Scientists do not fully understand the purpose of this strange appendage, but the age-old notion that it was used to loosen food from muddy river bottoms has been discounted. Long sought for their delicious white flesh, which tastes much like swordfish and salmon, and for their dark roe, which can be easily passed off as caviar, paddlefish were in serious decline during most of the twentieth century. They had been overfished throughout their range in the rivers and lakes of the upper Mississippi Valley. At the same time, their habitat had been reduced and their migration impeded by dams.

In 1932 the owner of the Allis-Chalmers farm implement company, himself an amateur ichthyologist, went so far as to offer a $1,000 reward for anyone who could capture a healthy young paddlefish so that he might study the fish's reproductive cycle. The reward was never claimed. Then, in 1960, a Missouri biologist accidentally witnessed paddlefish spawning, which helped enable fisheries experts to devise a hatchery program for the fish.

With spoonbill stocks now up throughout Missouri and much of their former range in the Midwest, a snagging-and-grabbing season flourishes in the Show Me State from March 15 to April 30 each year. Despite the sound of the term *grabbing*, nobody I know is stupid enough to reach out and take hold of a paddlefish with his or her hand. Legal size limits begin at 24 inches, not including the formidable bill, and weights average sixty pounds. The largest catch ever recorded measured more than 7 feet long and weighed in at 198 pounds (soaking wet, one presumes).

In view of these stats, the accepted and only sensible way to bring these fish in is by yanking a line, set with weighted treble hooks, through the water in places where the spoonbills are swimming upstream to spawn. A big fish fight then ensues, which the fish usually loses. Because these guys taste so good, catch-and-release is not normally practiced. Strict penalties prohibit commercial fishing for paddlefish or selling their highly prized roe.

The main rivers that are home to paddlefish in Missouri are the Mississippi, the Missouri, and the Osage. Because the Osage is by far the smallest of these habitats, and the one farthest upstream, some say it is the true home of paddlefish. An often-repeated legend holds that paddlefish are native to only two places in the world—the Osage River and one river in China. In fact the Chinese paddlefish, while similar, has a more cone-shaped snout and is in fact a distinct species of fish (*Psephurus gladius*). Hatchery paddlefish have now been introduced into several of Missouri's impoundment lakes.

The tiny town of Taberville in St. Clair County, once a fort on the Osage River, has a proud river heritage, and area residents who fish there will often proudly post pictures of their spoonbill catch where they work or in the local newspapers. You can see how paddlefish fry are raised at the Neosho National Fish Hatchery on East Park Street in Neosho. Call (417) 451-0554 for an appointment.

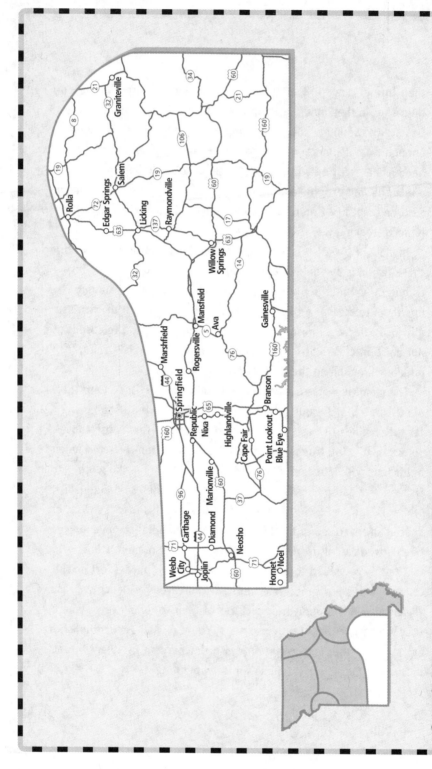

Ozark Mountain Heritage Region

6

Ozark Mountain Heritage Region

Okay, okay, the *Ozark Mountains are actually a plateau. If you are from Denver or Switzerland, you are going to laugh at us for call-ing these gently rolling hills mountains, but we do. And nobody who has come here to visit has gone away mad enough to take us to* The People's Court *over our semantics. Because we've stayed above sea level for the past 200 million years or so, and because none of the glaciers ran over us, this region has the greatest diversity of flora and fauna in the state. Most of the Ozarks were clear-cut twice in the past 150 years, yet when you drive through, you will be amazed at the long stretches of unbroken forests. Belowground there were once rich lead and zinc deposits, which made mining a primary reason for settlers to migrate here in the latter half of the nineteenth century.*

What we are short of, however, is topsoil. Rock-strewn fields and thin, porous soils make farming difficult. Being the poorest land to farm in the state, these hills were settled by less-affluent migrants, primar-ily from West Virginia and Tennessee. Wealthier and better educated people from Kentucky and Virginia bought better land north and east of here. As a result, the Ozarks had a reputation for being wild and woolly. For most of the last one hundred years, this is where you came if you wanted to escape from the law, or if you wanted to hunt and fish for two weeks without seeing a civilized human being.

Stream lovers still flock to the eastern part of this region for its abun-dance of flowing waters. Kayakers and canoeists can plunge through exciting and challenging rapids, while less-adventurous floaters cool their cans and chill their drinks while suspended in inner tubes on gently meandering rivers and creeks. Standing along the banks and wading through these waters are anglers after smallmouth bass and brown trout. Less sought after by sportfishers, but more highly prized at the dinner table, is the catfish, which lends its Native American name to one of the most popular rivers in this region, the Meramec.

Other natural features in the region include Grand Gulf ("Missouri's Little Grand Canyon"), Elephant Rocks (pink granite boulders), Taum Sauk Mountain (Missouri's highest point), Blue Spring (America's largest single-outlet spring), and Johnson's Shut-Ins (a dramatic river gorge). Here the U.S. government established the first two national scenic riverways.

The tranquility of the Ozarks was shattered in the early 1990s when the sleepy little town of Branson boomed and became the epicenter for country music and a flashy form of tourism. Now the region boasts an odd mix of hillbillies, retirees, show people, and tourists.

Lots and lots of tourists. And more than just a little quirkiness.

I could tell you about the quirky fella who legally changed his name to "They," so that when people say things like "They say it's gonna rain," he can claim to be the authority. Then there was the preacher who promised his congregation he could bring his mother back from the dead (keeping her body in a freezer and moving her around to evade authorities during his repeated attempts at resurrection). How about the town that ruled the head of every household had to own a gun? But you don't want to hear about those silly things. I've got quirkier stories to tell.

Ozark "Go Get'ers"

In most of America if you hear someone referred to as "a real go-getter," you can be assured he (or she) is a hardworking, energetic individual. The same phrase uttered in the Ozarks is actually a homonym with almost the opposite definition. An Ozark "Go Get'er" for generations has described a fellow whose wife hired on at the garment factory, the chicken plant, or (many years ago) the tomato canneries. That man might "run" a few cattle on his unfenced land, and certainly he hunted raccoons with the boys at night, but his main moneymaking activity was driving his wife to work in the morning and "going to get'er" at night.

I Had the Strangest Dream

Ava

The first weekend in June each year, the city of Ava celebrates Poke Salat Days. Named for the wild greens that country people ate every spring (some of us still do), the festival includes the usual craft booths, food vendors, and displays associated with such events. But the high point of Poke Salat Days is the annual bed race.

Five contestants make a team. One sits atop the bed with a stuffed animal, while the other four provide the power. It is not just a race but also a scavenger hunt, with teams searching wildly for things like a mountain cookie (think cow chip), a turtle, and cattle feed. I hear they now are frisking all the teams prior to the competition, because in a recent race the county's presiding judge was discovered

★ ★

trying to smuggle a turtle onto his team's bed ahead of time. (They are rough folks over in Douglas County, and they play to win.)

Take US 60 east of Springfield to Mansfield, and then go south 12 miles on MO 14 to Ava. For details contact the Ava Chamber of Commerce at (417) 683-4594.

Arms Spread Wide
Blue Eye

Years ago, when I found Pete Kibble's foot buried in a cemetery way up in Milan (see "One Foot in the Grave"), my readers responded with shock and awe, plus just the right amount of irreverent laughter. I never expected to find another storied body part buried just 10 miles from where I live.

As it turns out, back in 1936 a fellow named Kenneth Webb was working at a sawmill north of Blue Eye when a momentary lapse of concentration parted him from his right arm. The arm having served Kenneth well until then, he buried it with due respect in the cemetery on the edge of town.

Later in life Kenneth moved to Kansas, near Joplin. The arm was nearly forgotten, save by Mr. Webb himself, presumably, and schoolchildren performing their annual community service project of cleaning up around the graves.

Webb made an unannounced visit to his old house in Blue Eye, which was then owned by a relative of the teacher who supervised the school's cemetery detail. The teacher happened by and met Mr. Webb. Putting two minus one together, she soon deduced his identity. She does, after all, teach math.

Without a lot to talk about, she mentioned how visiting his arm had become an eagerly anticipated annual ritual for her classes, with each succeeding group of kids learning from their elders of the exciting revelation lying in store for them.

I'm not sure why a single arm should fascinate the children more than all the bodies lying there underground, but it does. I have been

told by parents and teachers alike that when the students are promised, if they are good, they will be shown the location of Kenneth
Webb's arm, "they will do anything you ask!"

Mr. Webb seemed pleased to learn of his celebrity status with the
children, and he stated his intention to someday return to Blue Eye
and become reunited with his arm. More time passed, and so did
Kenneth Webb. His daughter wrote the teacher here in town to tell
her how good it made her father feel knowing the children of Blue
Eye cared so much for him. Before he died, his wife confided that she
would be troubled if he were buried so far away she would have difficulty visiting his grave. Out of respect for her wishes, he arranged to
be buried in Kansas, but in appreciation for the children of Blue Eye,
he said he wanted his arm to remain there. I guess you could call it
the ultimate group hug.

From Blue Eye, on the Arkansas border, turn west onto State Line
Road. The cemetery is about a mile from town. Go through the gate
and take the first left. Kenneth Webb's arm lies about six rows from the
west end of the cemetery. The last time I visited, someone had placed
a small silk dragonfly atop the gravestone. Wave and be grateful.

No Nickel & Dime Business

Branson

Lots of people must have thought Dick Hartley spent most of his life
going in the wrong direction.

Coming of age at the end of World War II, Dick joined the U.S.
Army, and just as most of our soldiers were coming home, he went
to Japan. Once he got out of the service and home to Springfield, he
had to leave his young family to complete a management-training
program with the S. S. Kresge Company. In 1956 he accepted a man-
agement position with the T G & Y Variety chain, which moved him
to Oklahoma. Dick was getting established in variety store commerce
when America was about to fall in love with specialty stores, huge
mall complexes, and high-dollar retail.

★ ★

Dick and his wife, June, were nevertheless pursuing a dream, so in the late 1950s they created their own small 5 & 10 cent store in the sleepy little town of Branson. For a long time Dick was the only employee, even building many of his display shelves himself.

In the 1970s a competitor followed the national trend by going out of business, and the Hartleys seized the opportunity to occupy that store on Main Street. Some smug folks must have thought Dick had made a move in the wrong direction again.

Tourism was just getting going in Branson back then, but Dick's 5 & 10 fast became one of the most popular spots to visit. With an astonishing inventory of some 50,000 items, Dick's struck a nostalgic chord with visitors who remembered when a single small store in their hometown had just about anything anybody could want or need.

Housewares, sewing notions, linens, crafts, gifts, hardware, and toys; Dick's 5 & 10 seemed to have them all. And when your grocery chain back home stopped carrying your favorite bar soap or brass

You'll find 50,000 items for sale and countless
collectibles on display at Dick's.
DICK'S 5 & 10

polish, Dick Hartley would miraculously have those products too.

Unlike many such stores, Dick's 5 & 10 merchandise never seems
dusty or old. How they stock the shelves so full and so high, without
losing track of what they have or having it all come tumbling down
in a heap, is a mystery to behold.

In addition to the vast quantities of merchandise for sale, Dick
also gave space to amazing collections reflecting some of his other
passions. More than one hundred aviation prints are displayed, all
autographed by the aircrafts' pilots and crews. Autographed baseball
posters and other signed sports portraits give every fan who ever
lived something to cheer about. As if that weren't enough, customers
in Dick's 5 & 10 will see collections of arrowheads, model trains, and
a working Wurlitzer jukebox. All these things are evidence of

(Continued on page 178)

Country Music Mecca

Depending on how you look at it, Branson could either take up this whole book or should be left out entirely. After the Branson Boom in the early 1990s, a writer for the *Wall Street Journal* quipped, "Branson is what happens when white trash gets money." Previously Branson had been a sleepy little tourist town with a long off-season, good authentic country music, and plenty of Ozarks eccentrics. Some of the *Hee-Haw* crowd built theaters there and did quite well. The TV show *60 Minutes* did one of their rare entirely positive and uplifting segments on Branson, during which Mel Tillis was quoted as saying he guessed you could make "$6,000,000 in six months" in Branson.

Every unemployed and professionally dissatisfied fan of country music from Maine to California who heard that started dreaming of coming to Branson and scheming how to get here. Some began arriving the following week. Trouble was, that was fall, and the shows and restaurants were all closing for the winter. Branson suddenly had inflation, a housing shortage, a homeless population, and not enough of an infrastructure to cope. Somehow people survived, and by spring the Branson Boom was a resounding phenomenon. It became the second most popular tourist destination in America (after Disney World) and the most popular bus tour stop. Most of the tourists were of retirement age, and blue hair floated over the downtown sidewalks like the evening mists over Lake Taneycomo.

I live half an hour from Branson and (back then) a mile from my nearest neighbor. Soon the lights of Branson looked like the aurora borealis on the horizon, and I had Johnny and June Carter Cash as my nearest neighbors. (They used to swap me theater tickets for eggs.)

Branson has more theater seats than Nashville and more motel rooms than most major American cities. During the main season you can easily watch three shows a day for two weeks and not see any performance twice. There are three major factory merchant malls, dozens of shopping centers, and hundreds of little stores. There are more flea market booths than fleas on a pack of coon dogs. There are amusement parks, carnival rides, and loads of restaurants. But I sometimes miss the old days, when there were only two or three music shows and dogs could sleep on MO 76 because the few cars that came along would drive around them.

★ ★

(Continued from page 175)
Dick's belief that interesting diversions are an important part of the shopping experience. (It is a clever notion, evidenced by how many husbands contentedly wander about while their wives shop.)

One night in 2006, Dick Hartley locked up his store late, as was his habit, went home, and died quietly in his sleep, only slightly less than fifty years after founding his business.

Dick's 5 & 10 continues to be operated with a loyal staff by Dick's wife, June; son, Steve; and son-in-law, Dave Montgomery. You can visit virtually at www.dicksoldtime5and10.com or witness this miracle of old-fashioned merchandising firsthand by driving down to 103 Main Street. Open Monday through Saturday from 9:00 a.m. to 5:00 p.m.

I Don't Remember Privies Being Like This
Branson

If I am giving friends the whirlwind tour of Branson, we wait until the evening shows have started before we drive "the Strip" from downtown west along MO 76 to look at the lights. Then we end up at Shoji Tabuchi's theater on the Shepherd of the Hills Expressway, just off MO 76, to visit his ostentatious restrooms.

The men's room has a pool table, scores of black porcelain fixtures, and crushed ice in the urinals. I can't tell you firsthand what the ladies' restroom is like, but I did once see security guards escorting a woman out with the stern warning that she couldn't use her video camera in there. A lady friend told me their loo has roomy, mahogany-paneled stalls and a crystal vase with a live orchid on each marble washbasin. A uniformed attendant is ever at the ready to dispense a spritz of a favorite perfume or lotion selected from a wide array before the gals depart.

Officially the theater is at 3260 Shepherd of the Hills Expressway, but believe me, you don't need an address to find it. Shoji's theater has 6 miles of purple neon light tubing. Branson doesn't get any better than this.

Just Don't Stop Moving

Branson

The area around Branson has long been a nature lover's paradise, but the vast forests and pristine waters are rapidly giving way to bill-boards, highways, and buildings. One bit of nature that has survived is the buzzard roost. They even rerouted expensive new highways to protect the birds' bedroom.

In the valley below Table Rock Dam, next to the trout hatchery, a few turkey buzzards roost at night year-round. From October through

Vultures need to soak up the sun before they take to the skies.

★ ★

March they are joined by more of their kind, plus lots of their cousins, the black vultures, until their numbers swell to as many as 500. The scene at times is like something out of Alfred Hitchcock's movie *The Birds*.

The best time to go is early in the morning in winter, just as the sun is reaching the valley. Buzzards can't really fly well until their body temperature reaches a certain point, so you will see them perched everywhere, wings outstretched, soaking up the morning sun and waiting for liftoff.

The Missouri Department of Conservation holds a "Vulture Venture" every year on the last Saturday in February. They provide scopes so that you can scope out the scavengers, plus lots of games and learning activities for the kids.

From US 65 south of Branson, take MO 165 across the dam and down to the fish hatchery. Call (417) 334-4865 for details.

Kitschy, Kitschy Coup
Branson

Before Barbie and Ken, before Cabbage Patch dolls, before Raggedy Ann and Andy, and almost even before Teddy bears, there were Kewpies. It can be argued that Rose O'Neill's Kewpie dolls were the first major crossover from popular media to copyrighted toys. Kewpies started out as cute little illustrations Rose O'Neill did for magazines back in the early 1900s, but within a couple of years she was approached to turn them into figurines. A shrewd businesswoman, Rose copyrighted and trademarked all her creations, and almost overnight Kewpies were as thick as tribbles aboard the Starship *Enterprise*. At first they were sold cheap, given away with merchandise, and awarded as prizes at fairs and carnivals.

If there was ever a Queen of the Kewpies, that would undoubtedly be the late Lois Holman, twice past president of the International Rose O'Neill Club and a major moving force behind the Kewpiesta, Branson's annual three-day festival held the third weekend in April for Kewpie fanatics from all over the world. More than a thousand registered participants attend Kewpiesta every year to talk, buy, sell, and even compete in displaying their Kewpies.

Call Bonniebrook for details, (800) KEWPIES (539-7437).

The Queen of the Kewpies, surrounded by her subjects.
LOIS HOLMAN

Chicken Chores

During the years they played Branson, Johnny and June Carter Cash were my nearest neighbors, about a mile down the road. They loved their fans, but they couldn't handle living in the midst of all that hubbub.

Not long after they moved in, they stopped by my herb farm to look at the gardens. I gave them a basket of eggs I'd just gathered. You'd have thought I'd given them gold.

June ran her fingers over the still-warm eggs and exclaimed, "Oh, this takes me back to when John Carter [Cash] was little!"

She took a confidential tone and explained, "When that boy was little, he started to get too full of himself.

"I'd be darned if I'd raise a star's brat," the former child darling of the Carter family told me, "so I went out and bought that boy a dozen laying hens. He had to feed them, he had to water them, he had to gather the eggs, and he had to clean the you-know-what out of the chicken house.

"There's nothing that keeps a kid down to earth like cleaning out the chicken house!" she assured me with a wink.

Rose O'Neill's Bonniebrook
Branson

If you had all the money you wanted and homes in New York, Connecticut, the Isle of Capri, and Missouri, where would you retire? Rose O'Neill had all those things, and she picked the woods outside Branson. Rose always claimed that the house she built for her parents and named Bonniebrook was where she had the dream wherein the little Kewpies first appeared to her.

Although not originally from Missouri, Rose came to Bonniebrook frequently for inspiration and retired there in the late 1930s. Rose died at Bonniebrook in 1944, and Bonniebrook burned to the ground a few years later. Rose O'Neill's fans have rebuilt Bonniebrook on the same spot and filled it with some of her furnishings and other authentic period antiques. There it serves as a mecca for Rose O'Neill fans and Kewpie fanatics. In addition to the homesite, there is a museum, gift shop, and family cemetery. You can even get married there, if you wish.

Bonniebrook is 8 miles north of Branson on US 65. Open April through November; admission charged. Call (800) 539-7437.

Oinklawn Downs
Cape Fair

There was once a famous race between a racehorse and a pig, which the pig won. This would surprise no one who has attended Oinklawn Downs. The secret is to make the course fairly short with a lot of turns, which favors the pig. In the case of Oinklawn Downs, where horses are barred and the pigs are all trained and costumed by the same entrepreneur, you need merely select the pig of your choice from among the colorful and photogenic competitors. The little porkers run fleet of foot and with great enthusiasm for the Oreo cookies they receive as their reward for each race.

The festivities are held the second weekend in June each year in the little fishing resort town of Cape Fair; the chamber of commerce serves barbecue both Saturday and Sunday. (Chicken is available, too, for those who can't bear to put fork to pork at such an event.) The desserts served by the local senior citizens center provide an atmosphere similar to an old-fashioned pie supper.

In recent years professional musicians have been recruited from nearby Branson, but the open jam session featuring both amateur and professional musicians from all around the area has proved equally popular. Sunday there is gospel music all day. Add to this carnival games for the kids, a car show, and a street dance, and you'll want to race right back next year.

Cape Fair is on MO 76, west of Branson and Reeds Spring. For details call the Cape Fair Chamber of Commerce at (417) 538-2222 or visit www.capefairchamber.com.

Down the home stretch.
PAM SOETAERT

Maybe I'll Just Have the Buffet

For years in Branson there has been a local restaurant that serves pretty good food, but the reason I keep going back is the menu. The line "Soup de Jour, served daily" is followed by the generous statement, "All a la Carte Items come with your choice of potato, two vegetables, and salad bar." If that leaves you hungry for more, under "Desserts" you will notice that "Pie a la Mode" costs $2, but "Pie a la Mode, with Ice Cream" is 50 cents more.

I don't know about you, but I couldn't eat another thing—my stomach hurts too much from laughing.

The Crapduster
Carthage

Painter and sculptor Lowell Davis is famous for many things. Nationally he is famous for his cute little farm figurines, which are highly prized by collectors. Closer to home, near Carthage, Missouri, Davis is famous for having created Red Oak II, an idealized and fanciful re-creation of the little town where he happily spent part of his childhood in Lawrence County. The original Red Oak is now sadly just a ghost town, and Red Oak II has flirted with the same fate.

High taxes, a bitter divorce, and an alleged white supremacist group's renting of Red Oak II for a controversial event placed the attraction's future in doubt. Several years ago Davis burned his studio to the ground in disgust, saying he would never practice his artwork again. Red Oak II was completely closed for a time, and only now are new uses for parts of the large property being found.

But Davis's spirits are on the mend. With the support of his friend, Sam Butcher, who owns the nearby Precious Moments tourist attraction and figurine empire, Davis traveled to the Philippines and found love again with a restaurant manager from Manila named Rose. The happy couple have been living on the grounds of Red Oak II with a good part of Davis's extended family. He has eased back into his artwork, making signs for local businesses, which he calls "life-size sculptures." His favorite, and perhaps signature, piece flies over a truck stop northeast of Carthage. It is an antique manure spreader, to which Davis has added biplane wings and a plucky pilot. He calls it simply *The Crapduster*.

Everybody is waiting to see what Lowell Davis will come up with next.

Watch out for *The Crapduster* overhead at the Flyin W Convenience Store, 13011 State Highway 96. Visit www.redoakii.com for more information.

How Sweet It Is
Carthage

If you can't stand the sweet, stay out of the candy kitchen.

Just realize that puts you at odds with 400,000 visitors who annually make the pilgrimage to Precious Moments Chapel and Park to immerse themselves in a saccharine sea of adorable teardrop-eyed children and their fluffy little animal friends.

Precious Moments characters were born out of the imagination of Samuel J. Butcher. The Michigan-born, California-raised artist was so poor, according to his biography, he would often pick through a factory dump, scavenging for art materials. After attending art school, Sam joined with a friend in the early 1970s to launch a line of cards and posters at the annual Christian Booksellers Association trade show.

At that first show, Butcher's artwork was reportedly so popular with the crowd that other vendors took pity on the inexperienced young men and pitched in to help them handle the flood of sales. Soon thereafter, Sam launched "Love One Another," his first three-dimensional figurine, which was manufactured by Enesco Corporation. By late 1978 the first twenty-one of the artist's themed figurines had been introduced by Enesco.

Soon Butcher created his own enterprise, which ultimately regained control over licensing and production of his first little family of figurines, plus more than 1,500 additional pieces his fertile brain has spawned.

There are now collectors' clubs worldwide, whose members vie with one another for possession of the most cute figurines, stuffed animals, books, cards, posters, music, videos, apparel, jewelry, and ornaments. Eager buyers will find objects to celebrate every occasion—except maybe divorce.

The chief identifying characteristic is the characters' signature teardrop eyes, which make them all seem about to cry without quite knowing why. (I am reminded of the Italian women who centuries ago put drops of the herbal toxin belladonna in their eyes to dilate their pupils and thereby appear lovelier to Italian men. Only trouble was, when they went out in bright sunlight, they were as blind as bats. Unless they were hanging on to a servant, they would walk smack into a pillar or maybe take a header into a Venetian canal.)

Keep your eyes wide open when you join the throngs at Precious Moments Chapel and Park, because there is plenty to see. Butcher says he had a dream to build a chapel modeled after Michelangelo's Sistine Chapel, only with mainly Precious Moments characters depicting the stories of the Bible. That may be hard to imagine, but he has pretty much done that very thing. Outside you will find the old English-style visitor center, Fountain of Angels, Wedding Island, Samuel J. Butcher Museum, Royal Delights sandwich shop, and of course the Gallery and Gift Shop. I don't know about you, but if I spend too much time here, I find I just have to cuddle something.

A visit to Precious Moments Chapel and Park is free if you can resist buying any of the too-adorable merchandise. All attractions are open daily, March through December; limited seasonal operation during January and February. Check www.preciousmoments.com for details.

Take exit 18B off US 71, north of I-44. Follow the signs to 4321 South Chapel Road.

When Life Gives You Peanuts
Diamond

Statistically the kid was destined to fail. Born into slavery to a single mother and never really acquainted with his father, George was a sickly child. Kidnapped with his mother by hostile racists at the end of the Civil War, he was returned home, but he never learned whether his mother was killed or merely taken away forever. Education was not a guaranteed right for such children, but George Washington Carver was raised lovingly by Moses and Susan Carver on their farm near Diamond Grove (now just Diamond).

Excused from more onerous chores because of his frailty, young George was allowed to roam freely through the woods and fields near his home. He walked the streambeds and tended a small garden hidden in the woods. The land became his laboratory and a lifelong influence on his life.

When he turned twelve and was denied further education at the local church school, Carver moved away to attend a school for blacks. With great determination he continued his education and received a BS from Iowa Agricultural College in 1894 and an MS two years later. He became the first chairman of the Department of Agriculture at Tuskegee Institute in Alabama, where he is credited with revolution-izing agriculture in the South with his work on soil fertilization and crop diversification.

Over the years, until his death in 1943, Carver developed 325 products from peanuts, 108 from sweet potatoes, and 75 from pecans. Three patents were issued in his name for processing cosmetics, paints, and stains from soybeans. He was the first African American to testify before a congressional committee (on behalf of peanut farmers) and the first to have a national monument dedicated to him.

The visitor center at George Washington Carver's birthplace carries on his commitment to education with a wide variety of programs and events throughout the year. The site itself contains several educational exhibits, and walking the grounds one can almost see a small boy exploring his world with boundless curiosity.

For the prettiest drive to the Carver Birthplace, take exit 18 off I-44 east of Joplin, and drive south on MO 59 to Diamond. Go west 2 miles on State Route V, then 0.5 mile on Carver Road. Open daily except Thanksgiving, Christmas, and New Year's Day. Visit www.nps .gov/gwca/ for more information.

The Heart of America

Edgar Springs

Those folks who work at NOAA (the National Oceanic and Atmospheric Administration) in the National Ocean Service must have a lot of time on their hands. That's what the residents of Edgar Springs must have thought back in May 2001, when a bunch of them showed up with a passel of media types in tow. The entourage outnumbered the population of Edgar Springs, which, according to the 2000 census, hadn't hit 200 yet.

And Edgar Springs is about as far away from any ocean as you can get in this country. So what was the National Ocean Service doing there, and why all the media attention?

Well, if the United States were "a flat, rigid, weightless surface, and the entire 2000 population of 281,421,906 weighed exactly the same," they asked, "where would the perfect balance point be?" (OK, so that's what those NOAA guys talk about around their water cooler.)

Turns out the answer was Edgar Springs.

★ ★

This is actually a pretty big deal to the Census Bureau, which has been tracking such data since 1790, when a similar measurement, had it been possible back then, would have placed the population center somewhere around Chestertown, Maryland.

You can't get any more Middle American than Edgar Springs.
NATIONAL OCEANIC AND ATMOSPHERIC ADMINISTRATION

The population center has now been tracked for census data taken every ten years for just over 200 years. And not surprisingly the dots, if you were to connect them, have been moving steadily westward and a little toward the South (as older Americans move that way to warm their bones).

In 1990 the population center was near Steelville, Missouri, less than 35 miles northeast of where it was plotted in Edgar Springs. At that rate, Missouri might hold the title somewhere within its borders for another twenty years or so, but the popularity of snow sports, or the discomforts of global warming, will have to start to register if Missouri is going to remain at the center of things beyond then.

With the title comes an 8-inch, twenty-five-pound, permanent polished-brass survey marker. The whole thing is set into a huge concrete post sunk into the ground to keep souvenir hunters from stealing the trophy and throwing everybody in America off-kilter.

The designation has been good for souvenir sales (of things like gasoline and bait) in Edgar Springs. A surprising number of people want to go there and stand over the marker to feel what it's like to be in Middle America. Folks in Edgar Springs already know, and they've got better things to do with their time.

If you feel drawn there yourself, you'll find Edgar Springs about 20 miles south of Rolla on US 63.

If You Call It, It Will Come

Gainesville

The little city of Gainesville has been sponsoring Hootin' an' Hollarin' Days for more than forty years now. On the third weekend in September each year, townsfolk rope off the square and throw what locals like to call "one wingding of a homecoming party." But you don't have to be from Gainesville or Ozark County to feel welcome.

This is a part of the state where people look you right in the eye and howdy you whether they know you or not. And (you can't help but notice) all the men in trucks wave at all the other men in trucks. It's not a big, flap your hand like you are swatting flies kind of wave, mind you. These feller-to-feller waves are more like, raise your index finger off the steering wheel just a bit, or stretch your wrist a little in passing. People around here call such taciturn trucker acknowledgments "the howdy finger."

Hootin' an' Hollarin' Days was originally dreamed up "to preserve the traditions, crafts, and lore of the early days of the Ozarks." The Queen's Pageant on opening night requires contestants to appear in their best country dresses and charm the crowd with stories of how things used to be hereabouts. Judges select the Queen, Deputy Queen (you know, "should for any reason the Queen be unable to fulfill her responsibilities . . ."), and the Princesses. Contestants select Miss Sweetie Pie, which is an Ozarks equivalent of Miss Congeniality, only more sweet and sincere.

Saturday there is a big parade featuring Mr. and Mrs. Chili Pepper. "Cedar Pete," a pipe-smoking hillbilly character who traditionally competes in various ways with members of the crowd all weekend, has become so popular that in recent years appearances have also been made by Mrs. Pete, a passel of younguns, and apparently even a cousin or two. You'll enjoy plenty of live music (including great gospel singing), a chili cook-off, a wild outhouse race, a pet contest, horseshoe pitching, and a turkey shoot.

The signature events, however, are the hog- and husband-calling contests. Each participant has a unique way of being heard across the hills and valleys over the festive din, and you'll see some men whirl around nervously when certain wives pull out all the stops and shriek or whoop into the wind to call their feller.

Thanks to Gainesville's commitment to preserving the Ozarks way of life, you can shop at countless little booths filled with authentic arts and crafts. Between activities, feast on an abundance of fair foods, beverages, and snacks. Each evening ends with three hours of dancing to traditional mountain tunes played by an Ozarks fiddler and his band. And everybody knows Ozarks Cinderellas go barefoot so that they don't have to worry about losing a glass slipper on their way home if they stay out too late.

Gainesville is on US 160, between Branson and West Plains. Visit www.hootinanhollarin.com for more information.

These Rocks Don't Roll

Graniteville

Looking for all the world like a train of circus pachyderms, Elephant Rocks are actually something geologists call "intrusive igneous rocks." This doesn't mean they are a bother. It's just that 1.5 billion years ago, hot magma oozed and cooled deep underground, forming

Elephant Rock at Graniteville, Mo., in the Beautiful Arcadia Valley

PHOTO BY MISSOURI STATE HIGHWAY DEPARTMENT

Elephant rocks never forget.
MISSOURI STATE HIGHWAY DEPARTMENT

★ ★

these coarsely crystalline red granite boulders. Over time the layers of rock and soil above washed away, and exposure to the elements created the appearance of folds and crevasses we see today. The largest of these natural elephantine sculptures is the 680-ton Dumbo, which measures 27 feet tall, 35 feet long, and 17 feet wide. Good thing this Dumbo can't fly. The park's Braille Trail passes a lovely quarry pond where stones were mined for downtown St. Louis streets and levees. The red granite columns of the Missouri governor's mansion came from this area, and nearby quarries are still a source of red granite monument stones.

Elephant Rocks State Park is located on MO 21, northwest of Graniteville.

The World's Smallest Cathedral
Highlandville

Lots of people have been to that big St. Paul's Cathedral in England. You know, the one designed by Christopher Wren? But not many have been to Highlandville's cathedral, which is just about the right size for a big flock of wrens.

Officially named the Cathedral of the Prince of Peace, this littlest of cathedrals (according to *Guinness World Records*) might be mistaken for a stone shed or a smokehouse if it weren't for the half-ton, bright-blue onion dome on top. Inside, the church is quiet and usually empty. The pipe organ is, of necessity, also one of the world's smallest. The cathedral is always open, but you are not apt to be bothered or proselytized.

Originally the cathedral was maintained by Christ Catholic Church, whose priests are permitted to marry and hold secular jobs. (And between the demands of a boss and a spouse, who has time to be doing much of anything else?) Their literature defined it as "the world's smallest cathedral, yet big enough to hold people of every faith." Don't take that literally, because the place couldn't hold more than fifteen close friends at once. But it was a big-hearted little idea.

Larry and Darlene Jackson purchased the property in 2005. They generously allow the public to continue to visit the cathedral, and they maintain it as a site where people can conduct weddings. Call (417) 443-6185 for details.

Go south of Springfield on US 160 to Highlandville and turn left onto State Route EE. Wind around about the equivalent of three city blocks, but don't blink or you'll miss the little sign on the left and the left turn that takes you into a rural residential neighborhood to this tiny shrine.

Spooklight
Hornet

For more than a hundred years, people near the Oklahoma border south of Joplin have reported seeing strange lights that perform mysterious tricks. Variously known as "the Hornet Spooklight," "the Ghost Light of Joplin," or the "Tri-State Spooklight," the phenomenon takes its most common name from the little cluster of houses known as Hornet, nearest to where the lights are most often seen.

Sightings vary greatly, but they are so numerous they cannot be denied. Sometimes the lights are off in the trees or out in a pasture. Other times they will travel down the road, skipping over cars or stopping in the yards of houses. People have described the lights up close as round, spherical, or diamond shaped. The light may appear as a single ball or as a "necklace" of glowing stars. A single light may break into two, which move in different directions. Then, just as suddenly, one or both may disappear. A shift of the sightings seems to have occurred around the 1950s so that E 50 Road now seems to have more sightings than E 40.

Local residents have reported lights filling doorways or windows, illuminating everything inside. The color is frequently golden or "goldfish red" and translucent, but combinations of these colors with yellow, orange, green, and blue lights have been seen too. The size can be small enough to be mistaken for a flashlight or "as big as a

★ ★

washtub," as folks used to say. One old man was quoted as telling his grandson that the light he saw in 1910 was so bright "I could count the buttons on your granny's dress."

There are no reports that the lights ever harmed anyone, so folks who live nearby view them with some pride. They endure the frequent questions or requests for directions with good humor and patience. Glib assumptions that the Spooklight is just reflected headlights off the highway or pranksters in the woods are pretty much ignored. Locals don't care whether you believe them or not.

Since the horse-and-buggy days, families have made nighttime outings to watch for the glowing lights, and pull-offs along the Spooklight road are of course popular parking spots for young couples. Respected scientists have studied the phenomenon, and theories abound. But none of the ideas put forth, ranging from escaping gases to electrical forces caused by shifting within the earth, have been definitively proven. Many people say they prefer not to know the exact cause of the Hornet Spooklight.

For your very own sighting, drive to Lant's Country Feed Store at 9911 State Highway 43 outside Seneca, south of Joplin. From there turn right onto Iris Road and go about 2.5 miles west to State Line Road. Turn right (north) and continue through two intersections, then turn left (west). The Spooklight most commonly appears about 0.5 mile down that road.

Good Eating from under a Rock
Joplin

Years ago the Undercliff Grill & Bar was a general store. Going into Joplin from the south on what used to be US 71, people would stop for an ice cream or maybe an RC Cola and a MoonPie. Nowadays you can stop for a beer and the best hamburger anywhere around. There is a nice deck outside where you can look across the road to Shoal Creek, but on your first visit take a table inside (they can seat about

forty), where you can appreciate the earthy atmosphere of the restaurant built under a rock overhang.

US 71, where the Undercliff general store used to be, became
Old US 71, and then old Old US 71 (to the natives). It all sounds very
confusing, but the cliff has never moved. From I-44, exit to Neosho
(south) and go approximately 4.5 miles to State Route V. Exit right
and go about 0.25 mile to Old US 71. Turn left (south) and follow
this highway about 1 mile to the Undercliff. Take a look at that neat
old round barn on the way!

Undercliff Grill & Bar is located at 6385 Old US 71. Open year-
round, Wednesday through Friday 11:00 a.m. to 9:00 p.m., Saturday
9:00 a.m. to 9:00 p.m., and Sunday 9:00 a.m. to 3:00 p.m.

A cool place to eat.

Mr. Green Genes
Mansfield

Jeremiath C. Gettle can't remember a time when he didn't garden. Growing up with his family in eastern Oregon and western Idaho, he remembers being active in the gardens of his parents and grandparents when he was no more than three.

By the ripe old age of four, young Mr. Gettle planted his first garden of scallop squash and yellow pear tomatoes; by the time he turned seven, he was already a bit of a seedsman, producing his own "play" seed catalogs. It could have surprised no one who knew Jere back then when he later turned up at swap meets, displaying his countless little packets of hand-labeled seeds, carefully organized in cardboard boxes for all to see.

While he was still a relative youngster, the Gettle family moved to Missouri and bought a historic farm near the Mansfield home of author Laura Ingalls Wilder. From there, in 1998, Jeremiath issued his first "real" seed catalog, printing 550 copies in black and white. Keep it if you've got one, because I predict that twelve-page beauty, with Jere's colorful prose describing his first seventy offerings, will be worth a lot of lettuce some day.

The Baker Creek Seed catalog has grown to 124 glorious color pages, with a quarter million in print. (That publication boasts more than 1,300 varieties; the last time I checked, the Baker Creek Seed Store listed more than 1,400 varieties in its total inventory.) Baker Creek Heirloom Seed Company's varieties have been featured in (most notably) *Organic Gardening*, *Mother Earth News*, the *New York Times*, the *Chicago Tribune*, and the *Sacramento Bee*. The buzz among gardeners is, if you're interested in heirloom seeds, you have got to be on the mailing list for Baker Creek Seeds.

Underlying his quality seeds, lovingly grown and passionately described, is Jeremiath's conviction that heirlooms must be vigilantly protected and sacredly saved, particularly from big agribusinesses' headlong rush into vast fields of genetically engineered monoculture

Baker Creek's Jere Gettle often suits up to
defend heirloom seeds and organics.

crops, which some say threaten the very existence of fruits, vegetables, and other food crops that have been grown for centuries untold.

Other weapons in Jere's arsenal against the dominance of big corporate agriculture and what he terms "gene-altered Frankenfood" include the *Heirloom Gardener* magazine he publishes, and his family's Bakersville pioneer village, where they host monthly Heritage Day Festivals plus a huge annual Spring Planting Festival.

The Baker Creek Heirloom Seeds Web site describes the latter assemblage as a "community with fascinating seed collectors, renowned musicians, national garden speakers, historic demonstrators, food activists, home schoolers, western re-enactors, organic growers, gourmet chefs, free thinkers, Ozark crafters, trendy vendors & herbal hippies . . ." Jere's list actually ends there, but I could add to the list, if space would only permit. Suffice it to say, Bakersville festivals are the most fun, friendly, and diverse events I have witnessed in Missouri (or just about anywhere else).

Now often working with his wife, Emilee, and their young daughter by his side, Jere Gettle and his staff of family and friends have established a formidable Web presence. (The guy is no naive hick!) The Missouri transplant has even exported gardening back out to California's breadbasket, with a beautiful seed store recently established in a wonderful old Petaluma bank.

You might begin your visit to Jeremiath Gettle's agricultural enterprises by visiting www.rareseeds.com, but don't think that you've tasted the entire fruits of his labors unless you attend the annual Spring Planting Festival.

The Baker Creek Seed Store and selected parts of the village are open Sunday through Friday from 8:00 a.m. to 4:00 p.m., except major holidays. Call (417) 924-8917 during the same hours. From Mansfield, go north on MO 5 and follow the signs.

Squirrels of a Different Color

Marionville

I can remember my Aunt Daphne circling around outside her house, muttering that squirrels were just "rats with bushy tails." They would steal her bird feed, chew holes under her eaves, and wreak havoc in her attic. For revenge she would shoot them with her .22 and bury them in her compost heap. Aunt Daphne might have felt different about squirrels if she had seen the cute ones in Marionville.

**White squirrels are everywhere in Marionville.
Even sober people see 'em.**
JAMES A. SMART

★ ★

You see, they are white—pure white, with little pink eyes, little pink noses, and little pink ears. There are hundreds of them in and around town. Local residents claim that the squirrels were the first white settlers in these parts, having been here long before Marionville was incorporated in 1854.

Back in the late 1980s, when the white squirrels were getting scarce, Jim Smart launched a campaign to help the rare rodents rebound. With the help of the local Lions Club and others in the community, Jim saw to it that squirrel houses were put up, nut trees planted, and extra feed spread around. Ordinary gray squirrels were trapped and given one-way tickets out of town, and the white squirrels staged a big comeback. Now, as they say, "you can't hardly spit without hitting one." But don't do that. There's a $1,000 fine for harming any of the white squirrels or trying to kidnap a single one of them. And they officially have the right-of-way on all city streets. Aunt Daphne, leave your gun at home.

Marionville is 25 miles southwest of Springfield on US 60.

The Biggest Telescope You Can't Look Through
Marshfield

At some point, almost all kids growing up in small towns experience a longing to get away. Edwin Hubble was born in the little town of Marshfield (on Third Street) in 1889. When he left town, he didn't stop—at least not until he had traveled in his mind out past the Milky Way galaxy, through spiral nebulae, to the limit of the universe on the very edge of the ever-expanding cosmos. (From there, when Mom yells out the screen door for you to come home for dinner, you can honestly say you didn't hear her.)

Before Hubble began studying the nebulae that brought him lasting fame, he worked as a Spanish teacher and coached a championship Hoosier high school basketball team. But his fascination with the stars led him to work at the Mount Wilson Observatory, where he came up with Hubble's Law: "The farther away a galaxy is from Earth, the faster it is racing away." That simple sentence disproved one of Albert Einstein's theories, causing the great scientist to visit Hubble in 1931 and thank him. Not bad math for a kid from Marshfield.

The Hubble Space Telescope was named in his honor and launched from Cape Canaveral on April 24, 1990. Hubble's proud relations, some of whom still live in and around Marshfield, dedicated a one-quarter-scale replica of the NASA telescope to the town, where it can be seen today on the square.

Another entertainment in town is to wait and see how long it takes before some tourist walks up and tries to figure out where to put in his quarter and how to point the thing, not realizing it's a replica of a space telescope.

From the I-44 exit at Marshfield, take MO 38, which goes right past the town square.

Couldn't Remember Where They Left It

Neosho

Big Spring Park in the center of Neosho has long been suspected to be one entrance to a cluster of caves where Confederate soldiers are said to have stashed a large arsenal. Accounts vary, but some say that invading Union troops trapped a large force of Confederate soldiers inside the arsenal cave and sealed the entrance. Others maintain that the cave had other exits and that all the men and munitions were moved. Enough of the cave complex survived into the late nineteenth century that townspeople tell stories of children playing there and occasionally getting lost. After one such incident, in which two boys were lost and rescued, town leaders reportedly closed and hid the remaining entrance to the cave in what is now Big Spring Park, but not so permanently that it could not be reopened some day.

Controversial attempts to find the cave again were made in 1927 and 1947. One excavation in the earlier attempt uncovered the walls of an old limekiln known to be at the site. Each time work was begun to find the cave, it was subsequently halted by the city's mayor.

Some residents believed the cave to be a grave and therefore sacred. Brothers J. W. and E. M. Abbott, who were old enough to have left accounts of playing in the cave as boys, left the city of Neosho $30,000 plus a farm in trust to maintain Big Spring Park. Their wills, dating back to the 1950s, include the request that efforts be made to reopen the cave one day and maintain it as a tourist attraction.

Current attempts have located the first cave—an oblong cavern about 125 feet wide and 5 feet deep. Cave experts believe a larger cavern lies behind it, perhaps leading to the legendary Confederate cave. (Some geologists have even theorized that the entire city of Neosho is built over a cave larger than Carlsbad Caverns in New Mexico.) So far work is continuing, although some of the old controversy still remains.

If you are near Neosho, and a Civil War buff or a spelunker, you might enjoy a trip to Big Spring Park to see how this underground mystery is unfolding. New chapters can be expected several times a year for the foreseeable future.

Neosho is on US 71, south of Joplin.

None So Blind
Neosho

Like canaries in a mine indicating bad air to miners underground, the blind Ozark cavefish (*Amblyopsis rosae*) has proved to be a sensitive indicator of underground water quality—if we would only see. These 2-inch-long, pinkish-white (almost colorless) fish are born blind in a world where they have no need for eyes. Living their entire life in the total darkness of underground caves, cavefish use sensory organs on their head, sides, and tail to navigate and to locate prey. Their diet consists of plankton, isopods, amphipods, crayfish, salamander larvae, and (as if those weren't "yuk" enough) gray bat guano.

You would think that any creature that can live off bat doo-doo could withstand all kinds of ecological onslaughts, but the reverse seems to be true. Cut off their supply of bat excrement, or let too much soap suds into their water supply, and these cute little guys go belly up underground. Maybe it isn't such a good idea to pour the oil from the truck in the ditch behind the house, after all. Way before water becomes unsafe for us to drink, cavefish can alert us to potential problems by croaking. (And I don't mean the way frogs do.)

As you might guess from their name, Ozark cavefish have a limited range, being found only in caves of the Springfield Plateau in North America, which restricts them to a small area in Missouri, Arkansas, Oklahoma, and Kansas. Fortunately, before we succeeded in exterminating the entire species, biologists found out how useful they are. A program was begun to raise hatchery stock at the National Fish Hatchery in Neosho. Blind Ozark cavefish are currently still on the Endangered Species List, but efforts are under way to reverse pollution trends and restore their fragile habitat. If the fish are pointed out to you when you are touring a cave in southwest Missouri, you might wave and say "thank you." They can't see you, but they are working on your behalf.

You can also see blind Ozark cavefish up close at the Neosho National Fish Hatchery on 520 East Park Street. For more information call (417) 451-0554.

Sucker Days
Nixa

P. T. Barnum said, "There's a sucker born every minute," and that's a good thing, because each year on the third weekend in May, about 15,000 people descend on Nixa, intent on eating their fill of these much maligned scum-sucking bottom-feeding fish. People say the tradition began back in the 1950s with three or four men led by "cigar-chomping barber Finis Gold," who together would skip out on their jobs each year in order to "grab" suckers while they were spawning. (Grabbing suckers is done with a treble hook and should not be confused with noodling catfish, which is done barehanded.) Once you have a mess of suckers, and the oil is hot, and there are plenty of fried potatoes—well, you might as well invite the whole town. If the townsfolk let the word out, then people start coming from all around, and before you know it, you are feeding all of creation.

Nowadays Nixa schools officially close on the Friday of Sucker Days weekend. There is a big parade, plenty of live music, carnival rides, craft sales, athletic competitions, and of course all the fried suckers you can eat. If you are a good grabber, they are always looking for people willing to donate fish.

Nixa is south of Springfield on US 160. Call the Nixa Chamber of Commerce for details at (417) 725-1545.

Canceling Christmas Cards

Noel

I found no grinches in Noel. In fact, everybody I met in the tiny town seemed to have the Christmas spirit well into the new year. I'm not sure I would be so jolly if I had been one of the sixty or so volunteers who had spent the weeks before Christmas hand-canceling 60,000 greeting cards from all over the world with the famous Noel postmark. But apparently holiday happiness is more infectious than the flu in Noel.

This Yuletide tradition got started in 1932 when Postmaster Ed Rousselot came up with the idea of a special Noel postmark for Christmas. Soldiers stationed at Camp Crowder nearby sent their holiday letters from Noel, so people all across the country got an extra Christmas smile when they looked to see where the letters had been mailed. Kate Smith talked it up on her enormously popular radio show in the 1940s and 1950s, and the practice of sending Christmas greetings from Noel continues to this day.

Estimates range as high as half a million cards and letters sent from Noel at the height of this ho-ho-holiday hysteria half a century ago, but present-day Postmaster Robert Brumbach has done the math and doubts that the number was quite that high. He also took pity on his volunteers recently and introduced self-inking stamps so that it only takes half as many thumps to get the job done.

You can get the famous Noel postmarks on your cards by affixing proper postage to the envelopes and sending them all in a postpaid package to Postmaster, Noel, MO 64854. But it is more fun if you drive them down yourself.

Noel is 50 miles south of Joplin on MO 59, just 4 miles north of the Arkansas line.

Kate Smith made
Noel postmarks
· world famous.

Under the Overhang

One reason it's so much fun to drive your Christmas cards down to Noel is the chance to drive along the Elk River and under the cliffs on MO 59 south of Lanagan. There almost isn't enough room for a state highway next to the river, south of the old resort complex called Ginger Blue, but clever (or stubborn) highway engineers managed to squeeze the road between the river and the cliffs. In fact, MO 59 hugs the cliff face so tightly in places that you actually drive under the overhang with junipers growing overhead. When weather conditions are just right, there are marvelous icicles hanging down, but don't worry—the big rigs break them off before they can scratch the top of your BMW.

Incidentally, everybody wants to know where Ginger Blue got its name. Lots of people are going to tell you stories involving an Indian chief. But I met a woman who used to work for the original owner at Ginger Blue, and she gave me the scoop: He named it for the color of blue paint he used on all the buildings back then. People weren't satisfied with that explanation, so he cooked up a legend, which got way out of hand.

To drive under the cliffs, take US 71 south of Neosho to MO 59 (at Anderson). Follow MO 59 south to Noel.

How They Moved to Beverleeeee

Point Lookout

Swimming pools. Movie stars. Yes, the Beverly Hillbillies had it all in Cal-a-forn-i-a, but they never would have gotten there without Jed's truck. It's a car, actually, but converted to a moving van/pickup truck in the most ingenious ways. Almost everybody has a mental image of Granny stubbornly rocking up there on top.

The Clampett car is on permanent display at the Ralph Foster Museum, on the campus of the College of the Ozarks. The comic vehicle might be what brings most people in, but once there, visitors

Westward Ho!
RALPH FOSTER MUSEUM AT COLLEGE OF THE OZARKS

find an extraordinary variety of exhibits. There is a Thomas Hart Benton painting used as the frontispiece for *The Grapes of Wrath*, fine arts and collectibles, a vast weapons collection, an amazing array of stuffed animals, an extensive Ozarks collection, and much more. If you arrive too late in the day to see it all, they will welcome you back, free, the next day.

Take US 65 south of Branson to the first stoplight. Turn right and follow the signs to the College of the Ozarks. Admission charged. Visit www.rfostermuseum.com for details.

Ralph Lanning's Heaven
Republic

When I went looking for the Lanning Sculpture Garden in Republic, no helpful state or municipal signs guided me to the spot. But along a busy highway, where one's mind soon goes numb to the boring buildings and commercially littered parking lots, a tiny oasis appeared.

The statues visible from the road at first glance look rough and almost unfinished, but a little gravel pullout by the highway gives passersby a chance to get a better look and reconsider. A giant heart dedicates the well-mowed green space as the Ralph and Gretchen Lanning Garden.

Get out of your car, shake off the agitations of traffic, and wander over to read the inscription on the back of the dedication plaque: "If heaven is half as beautiful as here on Earth, I don't want to miss it."

From the plaque, turn and wander freely among the wondrous creations and marvel at them as their creator intended. Highway sounds subside. The ugly signs of commercial enterprise recede, as if a distant memory.

You are in Ralph Lanning's whimsical bit of Heaven on Earth.

I was lucky enough to stop by when Mr. Lanning was in his yard, working on a more mundane project of directing rainwater away from his home's foundation. The frosty morning had turned sunny and bright, and the spry retired carpenter made short work of the job. Now in his 90s, he has considerable experience under his belt, including years spent on Civilian Conservation Corps crews during the Depression and a long stint helping to build Stockton Dam.

When he understood I was there to see his sculptures, he eagerly abandoned his tools and led me on a tour beginning with his personal myth of why the Ozarks have so many beautiful rivers and lakes. For those not lucky enough to find Mr. Lanning with the time to personally show them around, there is a posted version of the story and statues of Mik and Ike, the dinosaur with two heads that spit out all the rivers and lakes of this region.

Intermingled with statues portraying Mik and Ike, and the various characters they encounter in their story, are a lovely little church, a tall crucifix, and praying hands, all speaking equally well of the Lannings' simple, devout Christian faith. Then there are statues and stone carvings evoking ancient Egypt. Other carvings depict birds and animals or whatever else catches Ralph Lanning's fancy.

Lady Godiva sits demurely atop her horse, while nearby a prurient Peeping Tom steals a furtive glance and giggles, even as he is turned to stone. Mermaids frolic by a little water garden. (I wondered if, perhaps, they might come to life on moonlit nights and help Ralph a little with his projects.)

In the midst of our tour, Mr. Lanning took me inside to meet his sweet wife, Gretchen, who is extremely talented herself at crochet, rug making, and other handwork arts. Together they filled my head to overflowing with examples of their ceaseless creativity. In their hands anything can be turned into at least something fun or pretty and often a genuine work of art.

Ralph Lanning has been "discovered" by John Foster of England, whose publication, *Raw Vision*, documents so-called "Outsider Art" from around the world. The movement, first described as "Art Brut" by the French in the 1940s, is described by Foster as "the art of those who have 'no right' to be artists and yet create works that are so

★ ★

Peeping Tom takes a long look at Lady Godiva.

powerful, original, and compelling that those on the cutting edge of art appreciation have hailed it as the greatest discovery yet."

A large crucifix, which Ralph Lanning tried unsuccessfully to sell with a bunch of his possessions at a local auction years ago, now resides at a St. Louis art museum. What nobody at the auction would pay anything for, the museum curators were only too happy to buy.

Today dealers and art collectors show up with trucks and eagerly buy whatever Mr. Lanning is willing to sell.

"But if I sell it all, what would I have to look at?" he asks with a stubborn smile.

Recently Lanning received additional television publicity for his statue of a naked man facing the highway, complaining (via a sign) about the unkempt business next door, which refuses to clean up what Lanning describes as a "rat heaven." The naked man disappeared, but the sign and the controversy continue.

Note: At press time, it was learned that Ralph and Gretchen Lanning had both recently passed away (within one month of each other). While the future of Ralph's sculpture garden is uncertain, his art can still be viewed at the Springfield Art Museum, located at 1111 East Brookside Drive.

Don't Get Footloose in Purdy

Purdy is the school system that banned dancing on school property. The ban was orchestrated by ministers who believed that social dancing was sinful and led to other forms of immorality. When challenged by some of the students and more moderate parents, the antidancing faction took the ban all the way to the U.S. Supreme Court—and won. (*Clayton vs. Place*, decided in favor of the students who wanted to hold dances at their school, was overturned by the U.S. Court of Appeals 8th Circuit in St. Louis. That reversal was allowed to stand by the U.S. Supreme Court on April 16, 1990.)

★ ★

Converting to Solar

Rogersville

You might stop at Olee Jobe's Springfever Nursery to buy plants, but you soon get distracted by all the other cool stuff. Olee's wife, Sharon, is a talented artist whose decorative painted garden art is for sale in their gift shop, and Olee is always working on something weird from materials he has scrounged from who knows where. The walls of their outbuildings are covered with found art, primitives, and garden sculptures Olee has made. But most noticeable are the many,

Just cut away whatever doesn't belong.

many large suns. A few years back, Olee devised a way to attack old hot-water heaters and pressure tanks with his acetylene torch, unfolding them into the most amazing sunbursts. He is typically modest about the artistry involved to pull this off. "You just cut away what doesn't belong there," he says.

I think Michelangelo said basically the same thing.

Olee's sunbursts sell for about $200, and he'd just as soon sell you a set of plans for ten bucks. (It is his attempt to get everybody more into solar.)

Springfever Nursery is open daily April through October. Take MO 125 south of Rogersville about 4.5 miles to where you'll see suns, even on a cloudy day. Call (417) 581-0850 for specific hours or if you just want to buy plans.

Coming Un-Henged

Rolla

The University of Missouri at Rolla is a serious engineering school, but don't think for a moment that those UMR kids don't know how to get a little crazy. Take, for instance, the time back in the early 1980s when the High-Pressure Water Lab was looking for a way to show off their stone-carving skills. The result is visible today alongside the business loop of I-44. There, squeezed in among campus buildings and a busy midwestern cityscape, is a half-size replica of Stonehenge. Accurate to fifteen seconds for calculating time and positioned properly for the next 4,000 years, this half-henge took only about a month for the students to cut. How much time do you suppose those ancient Brits wasted when they were building theirs, what with breaks for tree worshipping and sacrificing virgins?

When the final stone was set, on June 20, 1984, there was a solar eclipse visible from Rolla, which "was purely an accidental coincidence of timing." A *Playboy* party school would have planned around this, to impress the chicks. But those party animals at Rolla did arrange to have an even smaller replica of Stonehenge, made entirely

No virgins were harmed in the construction
of this Stonehenge replica.

of cheese, at the dedication ceremony. The official record does not
state whether this cheese-henge was eaten, but there is the entire
text of modern-day Welsh Druid John Bevan's invocation. It begins:

Dyro Dduw dy nawdd
Ac yn nawdd nerth
Ac yn nerth deall
Acyn neall gwybod

Just try to convince me that the guy hadn't been chomping on
cheese.

Take the UMR exit off I-44 at Rolla and proceed south to the corner of Fourteenth and Bishop. Stonehenge will be on your left, at the
northwest edge of campus.

Getting More Than Your Just Desserts

Rolla

"Where can I go in this town to get a good slice of pie?"

That's a common question asked by road-weary travelers when they want to get off the interstates and into real American communities with restaurants other than just chains. Teacher Mickey Hopson and her husband, Ron, must have had that in mind when they started their little restaurant back in the mid-1980s and named it simply Slice of Pie. A place where you can get regular meals from 10:00 a.m. to 10:00 p.m. seven days a week, Slice of Pie exceeds your expectations, come time for dessert, with about thirty-five pies on the menu. Considerate of everyone, the Hopsons include some sugar-free pies among the choices. (They also have good apple-walnut and carrot cakes, too, but it would be just plain perverse to go into Slice of Pie and order a non-pie dessert on any of your first ten or twelve visits.)

Watch for their "Pie of the Month" features, which are not on the regular menu. These unusual creations will most often be in keeping with a holiday theme, such as green pies in March for Saint Patrick's Day or red, white, and blue pies around the Fourth of July. When I asked one of the servers what the most popular pie was, she seemed really stumped. "A lot of people have a favorite, but they are all so good, I don't notice any special trend. If I had to guess, I suppose I sell more apple than anything else," she said.

Slice of Pie is obviously a safe bet for anybody who wants a slice of Americana. It's located at 601 Kingshighway. Call (573) 364-6203.

Model A Plus

Salem, near Licking

A man needs a hobby. Or at least that's what Lynne Borel thought after her husband, Bracy, built their cabin home on a beautiful wilderness hilltop and then announced he wanted to get a Model A Ford.

★ ★

Bracy enjoyed tinkering with that old car, so he bought another Model A. And, well, a man's got to have a place to put his toys, so they built a big barn. The barn had a kitchen and dining room on the ground floor, plus an apartment on the third, because the family was outgrowing the cabin when they had what Lynne calls family "get-to-gathers." But even with all that other activity going on, Bracy and their two sons' all-hours fussing with those Model As got the place called the Restoration Barn.

Model As must be magnetic, because soon there were more of the vintage cars and trucks, not to mention all the Model A parts that might come in handy some day. Other Model A enthusiasts started to come around to kick the tires, lift the hoods, and chew the Ford fat.

Lynne's brother came up from the great state of Texas to see what his brother-in-law was doing with Model As way out in little Texas County, Missouri. He was so impressed he sped back to Dallas and fetched a dozen more Model A enthusiasts, who returned with him in a convoy of Model As trailing up from the Lone Star State.

Lynne and Bracy had been putting out some fine jerky and barbe-cue at their Raymondville Grocery & Deli for years, so when the Tex-ans came to Texas County, Lynne put on a feed to show those folks how it's really done. A local television station got wind of the story and did a feature on the big ride and good eats.

Suddenly people from all over wanted to come to Bo's Hollow and have tours, especially if they could get reservations at "the restau-rant." Only there wasn't a restaurant. And tours weren't exactly what Bracy had in mind when he bought that first little hobby car.

But Bracy and the boys had already built a cute little covered bridge, and it seemed only neighborly to have a little old-fashioned gas station where the Model As could refuel the way they did in the 1930s. Nostalgia being contagious, sometime early in this new mil-lennium, Bo's Hollow became a pretty authentic little 1930s village where visitors can get a bite to eat (outdoors) and show the kids how to shell corn and feed the chickens. (That's a donkey, not a mule, and they'll explain the difference if you don't know.) Among the other sights are a mine, post office, "hoosegaw," barbershop, and (perhaps inevitably) an outhouse with a perpetually surprised granny inside.

If you don't drive up in your own Model A (or even if you do), you can get a fifteen-minute ride in one up along Ashley Creek to see where the Borels' ram pumps (simple hydraulic pumps) operate. You can even arrange to have a picnic packed and transported with you to eat at a lovely spot along the way.

You'd think it would take a village to run a village, but this is still pretty much a family operation, with son David "Grumpy Bones" Borel doing most of the meticulous restorations now and chauffeuring the rides up the creek and back in time. "Big Boy" Dale Borel is the go-to guy for barbecue and jerky, but he'd be at a loss without the fresh barbecue rolls his wife, Charla, bakes every day or the sauces Grumpy Bones' wife, Ellena, cheerfully prepares.

Tours of the Restoration Barn for serious Model A enthusiasts are by reservation, and only in the morning, before Grumpy gets too busy—or grumpy. Don't show up on empty, because the gas station doesn't supply gas anymore, except to the twelve or so operational Model A cars and trucks the Borels maintain and use on their farm throughout the year. Do show up with an appetite, however, because the barbecue, jerky, and fixins are some of the best you'll taste anywhere.

Bo's Hollow is very remote; it's located 2 miles south of Montauk State Park in a time-warped hollow where cell phones don't work. You won't believe my directions, so get them online or by phone in advance, depending on which direction you are traveling. People from forty-nine states and twenty-five countries have managed to find Bo's Hollow so far. They all seem to enjoy the drive, but some of them get out of their vehicles whistling the theme from *The Twilight Zone* or *Deliverance*.

Bo's Hollow is open 9:00 a.m. to 5:00 p.m. seasonally, on various days from March through Labor Day weekend. Days of operation will

★ ★

be expanding, but the best way to plan your visit is to call (573) 548-2429 or check the Web site: www.bohollow.com.

Food, gift baskets, and all Bo Hollow products are available Monday through Saturday year-round at the family's Raymondville Grocery & Deli, 158 East Highway B, Raymondville, along MO 137 south of Licking. Call (417) 457-6400.

A Colorful Artist
Springfield

If you stopped by the Corner Printing building on South Campbell in downtown Springfield to admire the colorful mural outside in years past, you may have seen a little guy in baggy clothes and a colorful helmet pedaling furiously past on his little dirt bike, happily singing. If you thought it was just some wheelie-popping kid, you were wrong.

The artist with one of his happy cityscapes.

It was septuagenarian folk artist Robert E. Smith, and that was his painting on the wall. The dirt bike was the way Robert liked to get around town.

If you had flagged Robert down he may have pointed out Elvis and Ray Charles in his mural, telling you what he knew about the times they each visited Springfield. The painting is sort of a Robert's-eye view of the Queen City of the Ozarks. Used to be people would give Robert $40 for one of his little storytelling scenes because they were charmed by his sweet, intensely sincere personality or they worried that he needed the money. Now singer Andy Williams owns at least one Robert E. Smith in his highly touted art collection, and not long ago Vanderbilt University acquired a series of Robert's paintings. His works also appear on the Web sites of galleries specializing in folk art from all around the country.

Although Robert unfortunately passed away in February 2010, you can always see some of his whimsical and childlike paintings for sale at the Keyes Gallery, 229 South Market Avenue, Springfield. Call (417) 866-2722.

A Hut for the Hungry

Springfield

Hungry folks have been gladly waiting to get into Casper's restaurant in Springfield for more than one hundred years.

Okay, the wait to get a table is lots shorter than that, and some of the satisfied customers weren't even born when Casper's moved to its present location in a Quonset hut on Walnut Street. But Casper's is one of those rare eateries that nourish your soul as they fill your belly. Generations of loyal Springfieldians, and other folks from throughout the Ozarks, have made the tiny little cafe a landmark well worth visiting.

The original Casper's was founded in 1909 by Casper Lederer, a young man who sold sheet music and then operated a fruit stand near the Landers Theater downtown. Customers responded well

★ ★

when Casper installed a secondhand Garland stove and began to serve hearty lunches. Back then the Landers was part of the vaudeville circuit, so over the years Casper's fed the famous along with legions of just regular folks.

Early on, signature entrees included sandwiches made with tender steamed hams and a secret chili recipe that continues to win awards today. In 1948 Casper's moved to a Quonset hut at the "remote" location of Glenstone Avenue and Cherokee Street. Customers eagerly followed Casper out to the edge of town. It didn't hurt at all that the new location was just three blocks south of what came to be called "the busiest intersection in America" during the heyday of Route 66.

In the mid-1960s, facing declining health, Casper coaxed his artist son, Charles, to come home and help out "for a year or so." But Charles warned his father he wouldn't stay. The two reportedly worked out a schedule that had them working different shifts—like many fathers and sons, they couldn't get along for very long working together.

A few years later Casper passed away, and Charles found himself the sole proprietor of the restaurant where he wasn't ever going to stay. He expressed his eccentric artistic sensibility by filling the joint with loads of old chalkware figurines, memorabilia, and kitsch, much of which today would get you on *Antiques Roadshow*.

In the late 1970s Charles convinced a good customer to come in and help with the cash register during the lunch crunch. Belinda Harriman's children were old enough that she wasn't needed so much at home, and gradually she assumed other duties until she became the head waitress. Belinda had just the right personality to soothe the sometimes temperamental Charles and charm the diverse patrons. Together with cook Etta Mae Buckner, who had worked for Casper, they made a great team.

Then in 1985 Charles received devastating news. The land where the restaurant stood had been sold. They had to move, but Charles's heart wasn't in it. Belinda sustained her friend and employer through those difficult months, finding another Quonset hut back near downtown. The move was ironically as crazy sounding as the move away had been years before. Downtown was in decline. Would customers follow them there?

Charles made Belinda an offer. If she would continue to work for him through a few years of transition, without more pay, he would give her the restaurant. He died suddenly, before putting anything in writing, but his son honored the spirit of the agreement. Belinda found herself with a restaurant to run.

She had gotten the same old secondhand Garland stove Casper had bought to cook his first meals, and she still had Etta Mae to help her. Charles had promised Belinda the secret chili recipe, too, but when she went to where it was supposed to be, it was gone.

Trying not to panic, Belinda began to experiment with chili recipes. She convened a group of regulars to judge her attempts periodically, but try as she might, she could not duplicate the flavor and smooth texture of Casper's signature dish.

With just a week to go before opening, Charles's son called and asked if she was sitting down.

"You can believe this or not," Belinda tells folks, "but he had gone outside one morning after the trash had blown over. A single piece of paper was stuck on his windshield. It was the chili recipe."

She didn't tell her tasting team she had the recipe when she tried it out on them. Their smiles told the story even before they congratulated her. When she opened a week later, with no paid advertising, the crowd filled the parking lot and went clear down the block.

Today the little Quonset hut at 601 West Walnut Street, bordering a gentrified downtown, still packs them in. There's a community table where you'll never eat alone and a counter where you get sassed by the help.

Casper's is open Monday through Friday 10:30 a.m. to 4:00 p.m. It's closed June through August, but the lines will be long again come September.

★ ★

Clap On, Clap Off
Webb City

I don't normally pick a fight with somebody's big hands, especially if those hands are 32 feet tall and weigh in at 110 tons. But somebody has got to point this out. Just because the *Hands in Prayer* World in Peace memorial is huge, well intentioned, and spiritual in nature

What are these big hands holding?

doesn't mean it is great art. See for yourself as you come driving into Webb City on Business US 71, north of Joplin. These big, pure-white mitts rise up out of a 40-foot hillside and tower above everything around. They are impressive for their sheer size, but they remind me of the first (and only) time I tried soap carving.

Now, lest I sound as though I've got a grudge against the sculptor, J. E. (Jack) Dawson, let me hasten to say that I do rather like his statue *The Kneeling Miner,* which stands near his more famous work in King Jack Park. (And, no, this is not some place that was dedicated to an artist with an ego as big as his hands. "King Jack" refers to the ore from which Webb City residents extracted vast wealth beginning in the latter part of the 1870s.) *The Kneeling Miner* is modest and gentle, and you get the feeling that here is a man who has worked hard, seen many hardships, and quietly persevered through it all.

Mr. Dawson, I applaud you.

Snap, Crackle, and Pop
Willow Springs

Fires sure snap and crackle, so after you get done fighting a hot one, you are probably ready for a cold pop to drink. At first that might be the best explanation you'll be able to think of as to why someone would have a museum dedicated mainly to firefighting and soda pop. But Fire Museum of Missouri owner John Mathieu defies easy explanations. This museum is all about his passions, and his lifelong loves just happen to include firefighting and fizzy thirst quenchers.

The former Willow Springs fire chief is the son of the first 7-Up bottler in the area. With a family tie to the soft drink industry, it was just natural that John would get hooked on collecting pop bottles, soda signs, and drink dispensers. Those were relatively cheap and easy things to collect when John was a boy, so when he became a real fireman with big-boy toys, fire trucks and antique automobiles seemed like more challenging collectibles.

Advance of the Armadillos

About twenty years ago, armadillos invaded Missouri from the south. Slowly they have spread throughout the state, becoming one of our most bothersome alien species.

The first time you encounter them up close they are kind of cute. The next few times you catch them in the yard, they are mildly annoying. By the time you realize it was armadillos, and not some drunk run amuck with a rototiller, that destroyed your lawn and garden last night, you are ready to kill. Even vegetarian grandmothers have been known to become vengeful savages when armadillos have dug up their daffodils.

You see so many dead armadillos on the side of the road because they have a defensive fright response that causes them to jump high into the air when startled. Whereas a possum or skunk will instinctively hunker down at the approach of an oncoming car, and thus be spared if missed by the wheels, an armadillo will leap up and whirl around, placing it at the perfect height to be struck by a car's bumper or grill.

If your insurance agent offers you an armadillo rider, take it.

Dead armadillos have become so common along Missouri's roadways, highway workers sometimes lay the stripes right over them.

At last count the museum had twenty-three antique fire engines and one old hose cart. John has restored about half the trucks, and the remaining ones are in various stages of repair. The oldest model is a 1929 Studebaker; one of the newest is a 1970 Mack. Most of the others are from the 1930s, 1940s, and early 1950s.

At this jam-packed, fun-filled museum you'll also see a large collection of old and new fire extinguishers, plus even more firefighting equipment dating back to the early 1900s. (Come see for yourself why a fireball can be a good thing to have.)

Then there is pop. Few places in the country have larger displays than John's collection of about 3,400 pop bottles. John is a fount of knowledge of the saga of soda, from the mid-eighteenth century to the present day. Did you know, for example, that Joseph Priestley created the first glass of man-made carbonated water in 1767 (prior to that, it was all natural), or that by 1920 the U.S. Census reported 5,000 bottlers in this country alone?

John has created another cool thing. He is building a Memorial Wall with the help of all the visitors to his museum—sort of a cinderblock guest book. Every visitor is invited to personalize a cinderblock with his or her handprints and name. The wall is already 9.5 feet tall and more than 150 feet long. Touring the museum and making a personalized cinderblock are totally free activities. Donations are accepted, but they go entirely toward museum improvements and expansion.

You'll leave the Fire Museum of Missouri with a rekindled interest in firefighting. You'll probably be thirsting to collect just a few old pop bottles when they turn up too. This place puts a whole 'nother spin on bottle recycling.

The museum is located at 908 East Business US 60/63 in Willow Springs. Visit www.usfirehouse.com for details.

index

index

index

index

about the author

Josh Young has won three national awards for humor with his syndicated "Dang Near Native" newspaper column. A former teacher and social worker, Josh was briefly coaxed out of retirement from do-gooding to run a local county health department. Now happily self-employed again, Josh lives and works (and eats) on Long Creek Herb Farm, which serves as the setting for much of his country humor. He blogs and publishes under the title "What's so funny?"